www.wadsworth.com

wadsworth.com is the World Wide Web site for Wadsworth and is your direct source to dozens of online resources.

At *wadsworth.com* you can find out about supplements, demonstration software, and student resources. You can also send email to many of our authors and preview new publications and exciting new technologies.

wadsworth.com
Changing the way the world learns®

About the Author

Gerald Corey is a professor of human services and counseling at California State University at Fullerton and a licensed psychologist. He received his doctorate in counseling from the University of Southern California. He is a Diplomate in Counseling Psychology, American Board of Professional Psychology; a National Certified Counselor; a Fellow of the American Psychological Association (Counseling Psychology); and a Fellow of the Association for Specialists in Group Work.

Jerry teaches both undergraduate and graduate courses in group counseling, as well as courses in experiential groups, the theory and practice of counseling, theories of counseling, and professional ethics. He is the author or co-author of 14 textbooks in counseling currently in print, three student video/workbook programs, and numerous journal articles. *Theory and Practice of Counseling and Psychotherapy* and *Theory and Practice of Group Counseling* have been translated into several foreign languages. In the past 20 years he has conducted workshops in group counseling and ethics for mental health professionals and graduate students at many universities in the United States as well as in Canada, Mexico, China, Germany, Belgium, Scotland, and Ireland. Along with his wife, Marianne Schneider Corey, Jerry frequently offers training/supervision workshops and courses for group counselors. In his leisure time, Jerry likes to travel, hike and bicycle in the mountains, and drive his 1931 Model A Ford.

Other books by Gerald Corey:

- *Theory and Practice of Counseling and Psychotherapy,* 6th Edition (and Manual) (2001).
- *Case Approach to Counseling and Psychotherapy,* 5th Edition (2001).
- *Theory and Practice of Group Counseling,* 5th Edition (and Manual) (2000).
- *Issues and Ethics in the Helping Professions,* 5th Edition (1998, with Marianne Schneider Corey and Patrick Callanan).
- *Becoming a Helper,* 3rd Edition (1998, with Marianne Schneider Corey).
- *I Never Knew I Had a Choice,* 6th Edition (1997, with Marianne Schneider Corey).
- *Groups: Process and Practice,* 5th Edition (1997, with Marianne Schneider Corey).
- *Group Techniques,* 2nd Edition (1992, with Marianne Schneider Corey, Patrick Callanan, and J. Michael Russell).

Jerry is co-author, with his daughters Cindy Corey and Heidi Jo Corey, of an orientation-to-college book entitled *Living and Learning* (1997), published by Wadsworth. He is also co-author (with Barbara Herlihy) of *Boundary Issues in Counseling: Multiple Roles and Responsibilities* (1997) and *ACA Ethical Standards Casebook,* 5th Edition (1996), both published by the American Counseling Association.

He has made three videos on various aspects of counseling practice: (1) *Student Video and Workbook for the Art of Integrative Counseling* (2001, with Robert Haynes); (2) *Evolution of a Group: Student Video and Workbook* (2000, with Marianne Schneider Corey and Robert Haynes); and (3) *Ethics in Action: Student Video and Workbook* (1998, with Marianne Schneider Corey and Robert Haynes). All of these student videos and workbooks are available through Brooks-Cole/Wadsworth.

Bringing it all together . . .

Gerald Corey's BOOK AND VIDEO TEACHING PACKAGE FOR
Theory and Practice of Counseling and Psychotherapy,
Sixth Edition

Featuring the new edition of the widely-acclaimed, best-selling text!

FROM THE COMPREHENSIVE COREY LIBRARY OF TEXTS AND VIDEOS

Theory and Practice of Counseling and Psychotherapy
Sixth Edition

Gerald Corey

FROM THE COMPREHENSIVE COREY LIBRARY OF TEXTS AND VIDEOS

Case Approach to Counseling and Psychotherapy
Fifth Edition

Gerald Corey

FROM THE COMPREHENSIVE COREY LIBRARY OF TEXTS AND VIDEOS

Student Manual for
Theory and Practice of Counseling and Psychotherapy
Sixth Edition

Gerald Corey

Theory and Practice of Counseling and Psychotherapy, Sixth Edition
ISBN: **0-534-34823-8**

Instructor's Edition for Theory and Practice of Counseling and Psychotherapy, Sixth Edition
ISBN: **0-534-37050-0**

Student Manual for Theory and Practice of Counseling and Psychotherapy, Sixth Edition
ISBN: **0-534-34824-6**

Case Approach to Counseling and Psychotherapy, Fifth Edition
ISBN: **0-534-34820-3**

The Art of Integrative Counseling
ISBN: **0-534-57636-2**

Student Video and Workbook for the Art of Integrative Counseling
ISBN: **0-534-57637-0**

The Art of Integrative Counseling

GERALD COREY

California State University, Fullerton
Diplomate in Counseling Psychology,
American Board of Professional Psychology

Australia • Canada • Mexico • Singapore • Spain • United Kingdom • United States

Counseling Editor: Julie Martinez
Assistant Editor: Annie Berterretche
Editorial Assistant: Marin Plank
Marketing Manager: Caroline Concilla
Project Editor: Matt Stevens
Print Buyer: Mary Noel
Permissions Editor: Robert M. Kauser
Production Service: Cecile Joyner / The Cooper Company
Text Designer: Terri Wright
Copy Editor: Kay Mikel
Cover Designer: Harry Voigt
Compositor: Thompson Type
Printer: Webcom

Printed in Canada

1 2 3 4 5 6 7 04 03 02 01 00

For permission to use material from this text, contact us by
Web: http://www.thomsonrights.com
Fax: 1-800-730-2215
Phone: 1-800-730-2214

Library of Congress Cataloging-in-Publication Data
Corey, Gerald.
The art of integrative counseling/ Gerald Corey.
p. cm.
Includes bibliographical references.
ISBN 0-534-57636-2
1. Counseling. 2. Psychotherapy.
I. Title

BF637.C6 C5725 2000
158'3—dc21 00-022465

For more information, contact
Wadsworth/Thomson Learning
10 Davis Drive
Belmont, CA 94002-3098
USA
http://www.wadsworth.com

International Headquarters
Thomson Learning
International Division
290 Harbor Drive, 2nd Floor
Stamford, CT 06902-7477
USA

UK/Europe/Middle East/South Africa
Thomson Learning
Berkshire House
168-173 High Holborn
London WC1V 7AA
United Kingdom

Asia
Thomson Learning
60 Albert Street, #15-01
Albert Complex
Singapore 189969

Canada
Nelson Thomson Learning
1120 Birchmount Road
Toronto, Ontario M1K 5G4
Canada

For my students in human services at California State University, Fullerton, with whom I have had the pleasure of working over the past 28 years. They have been instrumental in helping me formulate and clarify the ideas in this book.

Contents

CHAPTER 3

Establishing Therapeutic Goals 27

CHAPTER 4

Understanding and Dealing With Diversity 36

CHAPTER 5

Understanding and Dealing With Resistance 47

CHAPTER 6

Cognitive Focus in Counseling 59

CHAPTER 10

Working With Transference and Countertransference 103

CHAPTER 11

Understanding How the Past Influences the Present 115

CHAPTER 12

Working Toward Decisions and Behavior Change 124

Preface

In most of my theory books I devote specific chapters to presenting an integrative approach to counseling practice and a case example of the application of my integrative perspective. *The Art of Integrative Counseling* is basically an extension of these single chapters and is aimed at helping readers conceptualize the various dimensions of an integrative perspective.

About This Book

The Art of Integrative Counseling is designed as a supplementary book for those who have had a basic course in counseling theory and practice. Unless you have had a course in counseling theory or have at least read a standard textbook covering the range of counseling theories, you may have trouble grasping the ideas in this book. This book is not designed as a substitute for a text surveying the counseling theories. Instead, it is aimed primarily for courses in advanced counseling practice, counseling techniques, and therapeutic procedures. In this book I assume that you are familiar with the basic concepts associated with some of the major theoretical systems underlying counseling practice, such as psychoanalytic therapy, Adlerian therapy, existential therapy, person-centered therapy, Gestalt therapy, psychodrama, redecision therapy, reality therapy, behavior therapy, cognitive behavior therapy, feminist therapy, and family systems therapy.

One of the trends in the counseling field is the move toward integration of various theoretical systems and approaches to counseling. I believe an integrative approach is a more useful guide to practice. In this book I strive to do several things: (1) describe the concepts and techniques that I most draw from in my own integrative approach to counseling practice; (2) demonstrate how concepts and techniques can be borrowed from a variety of theoretical models and applied to the counseling process from the initial to termination stages; this I do by discussing my work with a single case of Ruth throughout the book, and also by asking you to imagine you are a client in counseling with me; and (3) suggest ways for you to think about designing your own integrative approach that will serve as a foundation for what you do in your counseling practice; this I do by asking you to put yourself in the role of a therapist at times and to assume the role of a client at other times.

I cannot tell you how to develop a personal integration that will fit best for you. I can, however, provide some guidelines to assist you in the task of considering which key concepts and techniques you might incorporate in your personal therapeutic style. In writing about my own personal synthesis, I am in no way suggesting that there is "one right way" to formulate an integrative perspective. Indeed, what I hope you will get from reading and studying this book (along with using the student video and workbook) is a framework that will assist you in systematically constructing an integrative counseling approach that works best for the person you are and for the clients whom you will serve.

About the Student Video and Workbook for the Art of Integrative Counseling

A new learning package, *Student Video and Workbook for the Art of Integrative Counseling,* serves as an ideal companion to this book. I strongly recommend that you incorporate the video and workbook to receive the maximum benefit from this learning package. Without both of these companion learning sources, you will be missing key information in learning about an integrative approach.

The 2-hour video and workbook illustrate my own integrative perspective in working with one client, Ruth. I make many references to the student video throughout this book. Indeed, in each chapter the central case example is Ruth, which I use to illustrate the concepts and techniques that are a part of my integrative perspective. I provide guidelines of how to best use the video and workbook as a combined learning package. The workbook coordinates a number of my texts with the video, and frequent references are made to these texts. The workbook—structured within the framework of 13 counseling sessions from the initial to termination phase—is designed to involve you in learning about an integrative approach through the use of interactive exercises and questions.

Both this book and the video/workbook have the same chapter titles (or session titles), which makes using the video/workbook and this book in tandem an ideal educational package. The format of the video for the 13 sessions consists of a lecturette on specific dimensions of my integrative approach, a counseling demonstration with Ruth, and a running process commentary of Ruth's and my work together. For example, in Chapter 1 the central focus of my mini-lecture is on how I draw from existential therapy, person-centered therapy, Adlerian therapy, and feminist therapy at the initial stage of my work with clients. Then, in the beginning session I demonstrate my application of selected concepts and techniques as I would apply them to the initial counseling session with Ruth. After the first counseling session, I provide a brief process commentary highlighting salient aspects that I most wanted to address with Ruth. The other 12 sessions follow the same format. Viewing the video and studying/completing the workbook as you read each of the chapters in this book will make for a more complete presentation of ways to create your own personal integration.

Many of my comments in this book are directed to how I would apply a range of selected concepts and techniques in working with Ruth over the course of short-term counseling (13 sessions). It will be important for you to interpret and apply what I write in this book to your own client population, as well as to the setting in which you work. The text and student workbook will provide ideas for doing this. Furthermore, although Ruth is the only case example I use in this book, I have included sections where you, the reader, can place yourself in the role of the client as well as in the role of the therapist.

A Complete Teaching/Learning Package

Case Approach to Counseling and Psychotherapy, 5th Edition (Corey, 2001b) reflects my increasing emphasis on the use of demonstrations and the case approach method to bridge the gap between the theory and practice of counseling. This book highlights the 10 counseling approaches—psychoanalytic, Adlerian, existential, person-centered, Gestalt, reality, behavior, cognitive behavior, feminist, and family systems—and demonstrates how each of the various therapeutic approaches is applied to the same client, Ruth, who is followed throughout this book. A feature of the text is an assessment of Ruth's case by one or more guest consultants in each of the 10 theoretical perspectives. Highly competent practitioners assess and treat Ruth from their particular theoretical orientation; they also provide sample dialogues to illustrate their style of working with Ruth. It is an excellent complement to this volume.

In addition, in *The Art of Integrative Counseling* I make frequent reference to my main textbook, *Theory and Practice of Counseling and Psychotherapy,* 6th Edition, which is accompanied by the *Student Manual for Theory and Practice of Counseling and Psychotherapy.* If you have used this book in a previous course, I suggest you review the theory chapters. If you have used another theories text, I encourage you to review the relevant chapters.

Acknowledgments

I am indebted to those professors and students who reviewed this book and provided me with constructive input. These individuals are Arnold A. Lazarus, Rutgers University; James J. Bergin, Georgia Southern University; Robert Haynes, Atascadero State Hospital; Barbara Herlihy, University of New Orleans; Patrice Moulton, Northwestern State University in Louisiana; Adam Blatner, Private Practice; Mimi Lawson; William Wheeler, Mississippi College; and Robert DeWinne, Tarrant County Junior College, Hurst, Texas. I thank Marianne Schneider Corey for her review of this book during the developmental stages and her contributions to the final product. I especially appreciate the involvement of Patrice Moulton's graduate students at Northwestern State University in Natchitoches, Louisiana, who participated in a class testing of *The Art of Integrative*

Counseling book, student workbook, and video. These students included Nabil Abouharib, Jamie Anding, Bonnie Bell, David Cosio, Samala Duffy, Mary Herrell, Mark Lafferty, Dwight Lenard, Lotus Meshreki, Misty Ryder, Kris St. Pierre, and Alicia Urven.

Let me express my appreciation to Eileen Murphy and Julie Martinez at Brooks-Cole/Wadsworth, who contributed in significant ways to this new book. Kay Mikel, the manuscript editor, has done a marvelous job of contributing to the reader friendliness of the book. Cecile Joyner, of The Cooper Company, coordinated the production of this book. Thanks to you all!

1

Beginning of Counseling

If you have applied to a graduate program in the helping professions, you are certain to have been asked these questions: "What is your approach to counseling? How does your theoretical orientation influence the manner in which you practice?" You will revisit these questions throughout your career—in job interviews and self-evaluations.

This book will assist you in the process of conceptualizing what you do as a counseling practitioner and help you clarify your theoretical orientation. I hope to stimulate your thinking about the importance of developing an integrative approach to counseling practice that pays attention to what your clients are thinking, feeling, and doing. Combining all these dimensions is the basis for a powerful and comprehensive approach to counseling practice. If any of these dimensions is excluded, the therapeutic approach is incomplete because no single theoretical model is comprehensive enough to explain all facets of the human experience.

I encourage you to examine the contemporary theories of counseling to determine which concepts and techniques you can incorporate in your approach to practice. Creating your own integrative stance is truly a challenge. It does not mean simply picking bits and pieces from theories in a random and fragmented manner. Each theory represents a different vantage point from which to look at human behavior. Study all the major theories, resist embracing too quickly any single point of view, and look for a basis for an integrative perspective that will guide your practice. No one theory has "the truth," but each may have something unique to offer you. Search for an approach that fits who you are and that allows you to think in a way that addresses thinking, feeling, and behaving.

The aim of this book is to assist you in acquiring a unique counseling approach that integrates the major theoretical perspectives with your own worldview. To develop this kind of integration, you need to be thoroughly grounded in a number of theories, be open to the idea that some aspects of these theories can be unified in different ways, and be willing to continually test your hypotheses to determine how well they are working. In developing and conceptualizing your integrative counseling approach, you need to consider your own personality. You must also think about what concepts and techniques work best with a range of clients. It requires knowledge, skill, art, and experience to be able to determine what techniques are suitable for particular problems. It is also an art to know when and how to use a particular therapeutic intervention.

Although it is essential to become well grounded in the theories underlying your practice, to acquire intervention skills, and to gain supervised experience as a counselor, this is not enough to make you an effective counselor. It is also essential that you be willing to take an honest look at your own life to determine if you are willing to do for yourself what you challenge clients to do. It will be hard to inspire clients to seek help when they need it if you are not open to asking for help in your own life. It will be difficult to sell others on that which you aren't buying yourself.

The best way to conceptualize your personal integrative approach is to apply the concepts of the various theories to your personal life. Furthermore, you will get many ideas of ways to creatively intervene with your clients by experiencing what it is like to be a client. (See Chapter 10 for more on this topic.) Along with the personal benefits of experiencing therapy, you will learn a great deal about what is effective in reaching clients. Toward this end, I will ask you to imagine that you are the client when I write about using interventions borrowed from various approaches. As much as possible, I will ask you to put yourself in the shoes of my client.

Additional examples of applications of techniques are provided in every chapter when I discuss my particular approach with a client named Ruth. You will get to know Ruth well in the remaining chapters. In many of the chapters I will be speaking to you as a therapist, especially when I discuss suggestions for developing your integrative approach to counseling.

If you have not read the preface, let me encourage you to do so before continuing with the text. The preface includes a number of specific suggestions on how to make the best use of this book in conjunction with the *Student Video and Workbook for the Art of Integrative Counseling,* which shows my work with Ruth throughout the 13 stages of counseling discussed here.

AN INTEGRATIVE THEORETICAL APPROACH: An Overview

This book represents my own integrative approach to counseling. I am not suggesting that you adopt my conceptualization of theory applied to practice. You will develop your own integrative style based on your personality and the kinds of clients you expect to treat. By describing my personal orientation to counseling, I hope to provide a model to help you design a theoretical orientation that makes sense to you.

As a student, you can begin the process of developing a style tailored to your own personality by familiarizing yourself with the major approaches to therapeutic practice. Then choose one theory to study in some depth and branch out from there in your search for an integrative style. I recommend that you study in depth the one theory that comes closest to your worldview, and use this theory as a foundation for developing a metatheory. Being grounded in a theory provides an anchor for making sense of what you are doing as a counselor. Without a solid theoretical foundation you are bound to flounder, and neither you nor your client will experience productive results.

Attempting to practice without having an explicit theoretical rationale is like trying to build a house without a set of blueprints. The foundation of a house needs to be sturdy and strong to support the rooms. If you operate in a theoretical vacuum and are unable to draw on theory to support your interventions, your attempts to help people change will have uncertain outcomes. Theory is not a rigid set of structures but a general framework that enables you to make sense of the many facets of the counseling process, providing you with a blueprint that gives direction to what you do and say.

As a counselor, you will encounter a wide range of clients with diverse problems. It is essential that you have an integrative framework that can embrace a variety of theoretical concepts and intervention strategies. I agree with Preston's (1998) belief that to accurately understand clients therapists must be able to appreciate them from a multitude of perspectives. Preston identifies several key questions that need to be addressed in working with each client:

- What is not working in this person's life at this time?
- What are the particular problems and causes that contribute to the client's present predicament?
- What does the client need from counseling in a general sense, and what does the client need at this time to be helped to heal, grow, and cope more effectively with life?

I draw on concepts and techniques from most of the contemporary counseling models. I then adapt them to a style that fits me personally, taking into account the universal *thinking, feeling,* and *behaving* dimensions of human experience. I typically challenge clients to *think* about the decisions they have made about themselves. Some of these decisions may have been necessary for their psychological survival as children but now may be clearly out of date. I encourage clients to pay attention to their "self-talk" and to ask themselves these questions:

- How do your problems reflect the assumptions you make about yourself, about others, and about life?
- How do you create your problems by the thoughts and beliefs you cling to?
- How can you begin to free yourself by critically evaluating the sentences you repeat to yourself?

These interventions help clients think about events in their lives, how they have interpreted those events, and what they need to do cognitively to change certain belief systems.

Once clients begin thinking about their problems, they often become stuck due to unexpressed and unresolved emotional concerns. I encourage clients to experience the range of their *feelings* and talk about how certain events have affected them. The healing process is facilitated by using techniques that tap feelings and allow individuals to feel listened to and understood.

Thinking and feeling are vital components in the helping process, but eventually clients must express themselves in the *behaving* or *doing* dimension. Clients can spend countless hours gaining insights and venting pent-up feelings, but at some point they need to get involved in an action-oriented program of change. Their feelings and thoughts can then be tested and adapted to real-life situations. If the helping process includes a focus on what people are doing, there is a greater chance that clients will also be able to change their thinking and feeling. Using an integrative counseling style, there is interaction between these three dimensions throughout the counseling process.

Another aspect of my integrative approach is to help clients consolidate what they are learning and apply new behaviors to situations they encounter every day. Some strategies I use are contracts, homework assignments, action programs, self-monitoring techniques, support systems, and self-directed programs of change. (These strategies are discussed in some detail in Chapters 8, 9, and 12.) These approaches all stress the role of commitment on the part of clients to practice new behaviors, to follow through with a realistic plan for change, and to develop practical methods of carrying out this plan in everyday life.

Ultimately, the most meaningful counseling perspective is one that is an extension of your values and personality. Developing such a personalized approach that guides your practice is an ongoing process, and your model will continuously undergo revision. A place to begin this process is by reflecting on your own values and life experiences.*

PUT YOURSELF IN THE SHOES OF THE CLIENT

The Initial Counseling Session

One of my goals in writing this book is to include you experientially in the process of organizing your perspective about what aspects to draw from various theories. When teaching, I do this by asking my students to place themselves in the world of their client. Likewise, as readers I will ask you to

* For an integrative approach applied to brief therapy, I highly recommend Preston, 1998.

"become the client" and reflect on integration from that perspective. To start this process now, imagine that you are the client and we are about to have our first session. As a therapist, I realize that the first few minutes are critical in setting the tone. Do you feel that way too? I begin by explaining to you the confidential context of our work together, including the main limitations of confidentiality. How does this feel to you? By explaining a few of the basic rules of therapy I hope to provide a sense of safety that will allow you to talk freely. To promote trust and rapport I ask you what you expected of today. Does this help you get focused?

What I most want to be able to do is listen to your story. How does it feel to finally share your story with someone? Meeting and valuing you as a person is essential to positive change. To create a working therapeutic relationship, I try to help you become aware of your assets and strengths rather than initially addressing your problems, deficits, and liabilities. During the initial session, my aim is to establish a positive relationship by listening, responding, demonstrating respect for your capacity to understand yourself, and exhibiting faith, hope, and caring. Here are some questions I'd likely ask you during the first session:

- What brings you here? What has been going on in your life recently that prompted you to seek professional help at this time?
- What expectations do you have of therapy? Of me? What are your hopes, fears, and reservations? What goals do you have for yourself through therapy?
- Could you give me a picture of some significant turning points in your life? Who have been the important people in your life? What significant decisions have you made? What are some of the struggles you've dealt with, and what are some of the issues that are current for you?

To the extent possible, I avoid preconceived notions about what our dialogue will consist of or how the therapy process will unfold. Instead, my hope is that you will share your present thoughts and feelings as they pertain to being in this session. It might very well be that you are not at all sure what you want from counseling and you may have ambivalent feelings about being in the office. You may be uncertain about how your being in counseling will change your relationships at home. This lack of certainty is a good place to begin. I want to give you a chance to express your expectations, hopes, concerns, fears, reservations, and doubts about making a commitment to the counseling process.

Informed Consent

Educating you about the counseling process, addressing your questions, and clarifying your expectations are routes to ethical and effective practice. The challenge involves creating a balance between giving you too much or not enough information. The main agenda is to provide you with the opportunity to talk about what you hope to gain from being in counseling. For you to feel trusting enough to meaningfully express yourself, you need to have at least some minimal information about the nature of the therapeutic relationship. What do you want to know about how counseling works as you begin as my client? What do you consider essential to know before you make a commitment to this professional relationship? Here are some topics we might explore during our early sessions:

- How is confidentiality essential and what are the limits of confidentiality?
- How does the therapeutic process work?
- What is my primary role as a therapist?
- What is expected of you as a client?
- What is the approximate length of the counseling process?
- How will termination be handled?
- What are your main rights and responsibilities?
- What are some of the main benefits and risks of therapy?

Let's assume, during this first session, that you say to me: "One of the troubles I have is trusting myself. I always think about what others expect of me. I've tried to please others for so long that I don't know who I am most of the time." This is a good lead for me to briefly educate you about a key task of therapy: part of the therapeutic journey will consist of challenging you to begin to examine the ways in which you think, feel, or act.

I am concerned about establishing an egalitarian working relationship with you. I spend considerable time explaining my view of the therapy process and how it works. By demystifying the therapeutic process, I am conveying to you that you are largely in charge of the direction your therapy will take. (All of this fits within the framework of feminist therapy.) The process of counseling will center on assisting you to look within to find your own answers. By refusing to provide easy solutions or answers, I confront you with the reality that you alone must find your own answers.

At the outset of therapy you have learned about the nature of counseling, the purpose and limitations of confidentiality, the procedures that may be employed, and the benefits and risks. How do you feel? Later in the session I will give you information about the specific therapy procedures I believe are appropriate for your particular problems. I will also involve you in the choice of techniques used in dealing with your problems. This practice of informing you about the counseling process is an ethical requirement that is part of the codes of ethics of all the major mental health professions. (Again, all these procedures are an integral part of feminist therapy.) Does this help you feel informed? Fully enfranchised? A partner in the therapeutic venture?

Assessment

Still in the first session, I begin the process of conducting an assessment and sharing my impressions with you. I am likely to employ an Adlerian technique as part of your assessment that Dreikurs (1997) called *The Question:* "How would your life be different if you did not have this problem? What would you do differently if you did not have this symptom or problem?" If you state that nothing would be different, especially with physical symptoms, I would suspect that the problem may be organic and require medical intervention. However, if you say that "if it weren't for this depression, I would get out more and see my friends," I might think you are avoiding something you perceive as necessary but from which you wish to retreat. Such a statement may reveal your concern about the possibility of being a good friend or being welcomed by your friends. Raising such questions can be a good catalyst to stimulate your reflection on what it might be like for you if you were able to change some problematic area in your life.

Therapy Is a Time-Limited Process

Do you want short-term counseling or longer term counseling? If you are my client in a setting where brief therapy is the standard, it is especially important for me to be clear about the number of sessions allowed. If an agency policy specifies that you can be seen for only six sessions, you have a right to know this from the onset. Working in a short-term therapy approach, the final phase of the counseling process is always in the background. The goal is to teach you, as quickly and efficiently as possible, the coping skills you need to live in self-directed ways. How do you feel about these constraints?

The limitation of time can actually assist both you and me in establishing short-term, realistic goals. Toward the end of each session I will ask you the degree to which you see yourself reaching the goals you have established. By reviewing the course of treatment, you are in a position to identify what is and is not working for you in the counseling process. Each session can be assessed in light of having a specific number of sessions devoted to accomplishing preset goals.

My overriding goal is to increase the chances that you will not continue to need a therapist. If I do my work well, eventually I hope to put myself out of business. Thus, I am open to exploring termination issues with you at any point during the counseling process. Do you want to know about these matters from the start? Do you think discussing termination early on is helpful to you?

INTRODUCTION TO THE CASE OF RUTH

See Session 1 (Beginning of Counseling) of the *Student Video and Workbook for the Art of Integrative Counseling.*

Let's switch perspectives now and talk about how the case of Ruth can inform your process of developing your integrative approach to therapy.

Ruth's case is the primary example throughout this book, and she is the client in the video. Ruth is a 39-year-old married woman with four teenagers, coming to therapy for the first time with some anxiety and a host of somatic complaints. She lives with her husband (John, 45) and their children (Rob, 19; Jennifer, 18; Susan, 17; and Adam, 16). Here is a brief summary of data taken from Ruth's intake form.

PSYCHOSOCIAL HISTORY. Ruth is the oldest of four children. Her father is a fundamentalist minister, and her mother is a housewife. She describes her father as distant, authoritarian, and rigid; as a child, her relationship with him was one of unquestioning, fearful adherence to his rules and standards. She remembers her mother as being critical, and Ruth thought she could never do enough to please her mother. At other times her mother was supportive. The family demonstrated little affection. In many ways Ruth took on the role of caring for her younger brother and sisters, largely in the hope of winning the approval of her parents. When she attempted to have any kind of fun, she encountered her father's disapproval and outright scorn. To a large extent this pattern of taking care of others has extended throughout her life.

Would you want other information here? If so, what?

PRESENTING PROBLEM. Ruth reports general dissatisfaction with her life, seeing it as rather uneventful and predictable. She feels some panic over reaching the age of 39, wondering where the years have gone. For two years she has been troubled with a range of psychosomatic complaints, including sleep disturbances, anxiety, dizziness, heart palpitations, and headaches. At times she has to push herself to leave the house. Ruth complains that she cries easily over trivial matters, often feels depressed, and does not like her body.

Ruth has recently become aware that she lives for others. She realizes that she plays a role of superwoman in all aspects of her life. She feels that she gives and gives in all of her relationships, to the point that she feels empty. Ruth does have a difficult time asking others to attend to her. She tries to be the good wife and good mother that her family expects her to be—and that she expects herself to be. In most respects, Ruth does not like herself. She does not like her looks or her body, and she worries about what her family of origin expects of her. Ruth goes to church every Sunday, but she has left her father's church, which is the source of some guilt for her. Although her parents have not disowned her, it sometimes feels that they have.

As a counselor, what are you focusing on so far?

HISTORY OF PRESENTING PROBLEM. Ruth's major career was as homemaker and mother until her children became adolescents. She then entered college part time and obtained a bachelor's degree. She recently graduated from college as an elementary education major, and she is now working on her teaching credential. She does look forward to becoming an elementary school teacher, yet she often feels so overwhelmed that she wonders if she will ever reach her career goals.

Through her contacts with others at the university she became aware of how she has limited herself, how she has fostered her family's dependence on her, and how frightened she is of branching out from her roles as mother and wife. Ruth completed a course in introduction to counseling that encouraged her to look at the direction of her own life. This course and her experiences with fellow students acted as a catalyst in getting her to take an honest look at her life. Ruth is not clear at this point who she is, apart from being a mother, a wife, and a student. She realizes that she does not have a good sense of what she wants for herself and that she typically lives up to what others in her life want for her.

If you could ask Ruth one question, what would it be?

DRAWING ON THEORIES AS APPLIED TO THE CASE OF RUTH

Let's shift perspectives again and discuss how I would draw on different theories to work with Ruth. The resources I will tap as I counsel Ruth are from four different general categories of theoretical models of counseling. First are the *psychodynamic approaches,* which include psychoanalytic therapy, object-relations approaches, and Adlerian therapy. Although Adlerian theory differs from psychoanalytic theory in many respects, it can broadly be considered an analytic perspective. The second category comprises the *experiential* and *relationship-oriented therapies,* which include the existential approach, the person-centered approach, Gestalt therapy, and psychodrama. Third are the *action-oriented therapies,* which include behavior therapy, rational emotive behavior therapy, cognitive therapy, reality therapy, and redecision therapy (or transactional analysis). These are sometimes known generally as cognitive behavioral approaches. The fourth general approach is the *systems perspective,* of which feminist therapy and family therapy are a part. The systems orientation stresses the importance of understanding individuals in the context of the surroundings that influence their development.

My integrative approach to counseling is based on key concepts from aspects of all four general approaches and on techniques from each of the specific therapeutic models. This will become evident as you study the counseling sessions with Ruth in the *Student Video and Workbook for the Art of Integrative Counseling.*

THEORIES DURING THE EARLY STAGE. During the early phase of counseling, I personally find several theories most useful. At the beginning of the counseling relationship, my concern is to establish a foundation that will provide safety for clients to be able to undertake the risks necessary in making fundamental life changes. The basic concepts that I find particularly useful at this time are part of the experiential therapies, especially person-centered and existential therapy.

I incorporate many basic constructs from the person-centered approach in my therapeutic style. For example, I believe Ruth will tell me a great deal about what she wants from life if I can really listen with deep understanding. Although I see my style as being active and directive, I first and foremost want to see the world from Ruth's vantage point. Ruth will offer rich clues and provide me with leads if only I care enough to listen and observe. From the person-centered approach I value the emphasis on striving to experience Ruth's world from the subjective perspective and trusting in her basic wisdom. This approach gives priority to the quality of our relationship, which I believe is the curative factor that brings about healing and change.

In Chapter 2 I'll have a lot more to say about the central role of the therapeutic relationship as a determinant of therapeutic outcomes. For now, let me say that I want to approach meeting Ruth with as much presence, openness, and interest as I am able to bring to the initial encounter. What I most want to do is *assist Ruth in creating her own agenda* rather than being too quick to present my agenda to her.

Let me share my thoughts about Ruth's first counseling session. Early in the session she lets me know that she is nervous in coming to her first counseling session. She does not know what to expect. Ruth lets me know that she feels confused about what she really wants for herself and what kind of life she most wants. Her hope is that I will tell her what to do so that she can go and do it and then feel better. She expects that I will give her guidance, at the very least, and would like it if I were to give her advice and tell her what to do with her life. She is putting me in the place of the expert and, in doing so, is minimizing her personal power to make meaningful decisions herself. Although I can appreciate her anxiety and lack of faith in her own ability to take an active stance toward life, I do not serve her well if I make decisions about her life for her. I believe Ruth has the capacity to identify what she wants in her life and that she can chart her own course. (This is consistent with the philosophy of person-centered therapy and feminist therapy.)

At our initial meeting I do not have a clear idea of where our journey together will take us, for much depends on *how far* Ruth wants to go and *what* she is willing to explore. I start by giving Ruth a chance to say how she feels about coming to the initial session, and I ask some of these questions:

- What prompted you to call and come in for this appointment?
- What is going on in your life that you particularly like?
- What do you want me to know about you?
- In what areas is your life going well?
- What areas of your life do you wish were different?
- What were you experiencing as you were getting ready to come to this session?

Of course I would take care not to bombard her with too many questions too fast.

Questions such as these give a flavor of ways to open the discussion of what Ruth is experiencing as she makes her first contact with me. These questions are central to the assessment process, which begins during the initial session. A guiding question in the back of my mind during this assessment of Ruth is "What does this client most need to understand about herself to grow and to deal more effectively with her present relationships?"

From our initial session I learn that Ruth has decided to seek individual counseling to explore several areas of her life.

- A physician whom she consulted could find no organic or medical basis for her physical symptoms and recommended personal therapy. In her words, her major symptoms are these: "I sometimes feel very panicky, especially at night when I'm trying to sleep. Sometimes I'll wake up and find it difficult to breathe, my heart will be pounding, and I'll break out in a cold sweat. I toss and turn trying to relax, and instead I feel tense and worry a lot about many little things. It's hard for me to turn off these thoughts. Then during the day I'm so tired I can hardly function, and I find that lately I cry very easily if even minor things go wrong."
- Ruth's four children range in age from 16 to 19, and all of them are now finding more of their satisfactions outside the family and the home and are spending increasing time with their friends. Ruth sees these changes and is concerned about "losing" them. She is having particular problems with her daughter Jennifer, and she is at a loss as to how to deal with Jennifer's rebellion. In general, Ruth feels very much unappreciated by her children.
- In thinking about her future, Ruth is not really sure who or what she wants to become. She would like to develop a sense of herself apart from the expectations of others. Ruth does not find her relationship with her husband, John, at all satisfactory. He appears to be resisting her attempts to make changes and prefers that she remain as she was. Ruth is anxious over the prospect of challenging this relationship, fearing that if she does she might end up alone.
- Lately, Ruth is experiencing more concern over aging and losing her "looks."

All of these factors combined have provided the motivation for her to take the necessary steps to initiate individual therapy. Perhaps the greatest catalyst that triggered her to come for therapy is the increase of her physical symptoms and her anxiety.

ANXIETY OVER BEGINNING COUNSELING. It is to be expected that Ruth has some anxiety about initiating therapy. I want to provide her with the opportunity to talk about what it is like for her to come to the office today. That in itself provides the direction for much of our session. I surely want to get an idea of what has brought her to therapy. What is going on in her life that motivates her to seek therapy? What does she most hope for as a result of this venture? I structure the initial session so that she can talk about her expectations and about her fears, hopes, and ambivalent feelings.

Because Ruth's trust in me will be an important part of the therapy process, I give her the chance to ask me how I will work with her. I do not believe in making therapy into a mysterious adventure. Ruth will get more from her therapy if she knows how it works, if she knows the nature of her responsibilities and mine, and if she is clear on what she wants from this process. (These basic concepts are all derived from several theoretical approaches, especially from models such as Adlerian therapy, behavior therapy, cognitive behavior therapy, reality therapy, and feminist therapy.)

Feminist therapy in particular offers a number of key concepts that can be incorporated in the early phases of the therapeutic endeavor. The feminist perspective is grounded on the assumption that the client is an expert in her own life. In working with Ruth I want to reinforce this idea. This is not to minimize my expertise as a healer, but I must always remember that my interventions are to be guided by what Ruth wants for herself, not what I think Ruth should want or my vision of her ideal life. To help Ruth sort out conflicting beliefs about the roles she plays, her therapy might include a gender-role analysis so that she can come to a fuller understanding of the limiting roles she has uncritically accepted. With this expanded awareness, Ruth can assume the power to make choices about the roles she wants to accept or modify.

Other elements of feminist therapy that I especially appreciate include the role of informed consent, educating clients about the process, and doing what is possible to establish a collaborative working alliance. It is important that I not misuse the power I have as a professional helper. I must truly secure Ruth's informed consent, and in doing so convey to her the expectation that she will be in charge of much of what we do in the sessions. She will be an active agent and make decisions at every juncture. I will not keep Ruth in the dark about how therapy works or about my interventions. The feminist approach teaches me how essential it is to demystify therapy. Ultimately, my hope is that Ruth will be empowered to become her own counselor. My interventions and my role will be to help her acquire the tools necessary to actively shape the events of her life and to actively engage in directing her own life.

THE THERAPEUTIC CONTRACT. As I begin formulating a working contract, one that will give some direction to our sessions, I discuss what I see as my main responsibilities and functions, as well as Ruth's responsibilities in the process. I want her to know at the outset that I expect her to be an active party in this relationship, and I tell her that I function in an active and directive way. (This is characteristic of most of the cognitive behavioral and action-oriented therapies.)

I see therapy as a significant project—an investment in the self, if you will—and I think Ruth has a right to know about both the potential benefits and the risks of her becoming a counseling client. Early in the counseling process it is essential that I get some sense of what Ruth wants from counseling and life. Although her responses are vague at first, I work with her to become as specific and concrete as possible regarding how she views her life situation and what she expects from the therapy process. (This process is especially important in Adlerian therapy, behavior therapy, cognitive behavior therapy, reality therapy, and feminist therapy. I will further discuss goals in Chapter 3.)

LETTING RUTH TELL HER STORY. Counselors often receive information about clients before meeting them for the first time. These data may have been gathered in an intake or as part of a referral process. However, I do not begin by gathering life-history data, though I do think this is important. I want to make person-to-person contact with Ruth rather than starting with "her problem." Even if Ruth surfaces her concerns in therapy rather quickly, the initial attention should be on her, not the presenting problem. I see value in first letting Ruth tell her story in the way she chooses. How she walks into the office, her tone of voice, postures, facial expressions, gestures, hesitations in speech, nonverbal language, mannerisms, and style of speech are all of interest to me. The details Ruth chooses to go into, and what she decides to relate and not to relate, provide me with a valuable perspective from which to understand her. I am interested in how Ruth perceives the events in her life and how she feels in her subjective world. (This concept of understanding the phenomenological world of the client is especially important in the existential, person-centered, and Adlerian models.) Let me stress that there will be limited time for Ruth to share her story during the first session. This process can begin, yet it will take several sessions for her to reveal key themes in her life.

If I do too much structuring initially, I interfere with her typical style of presenting herself. I strive to listen carefully and to let her know what I am hearing. (Person-centered therapists place this at the core of therapy.) Understanding the client's world is something I especially value in the initial stages of therapy. I want to avoid the tendency to talk too much during this initial session. Being fully present in the therapy session and giving Ruth my sincere attention will pay rich dividends in terms of the potential for therapy. If I listen well, I will get a good sense of why she is coming to therapy. If I fail to listen accurately and sensitively, there is a risk of going with the first problem she states instead of waiting and listening to discover the depth of her experience. If I am too eager to help, I might try too hard to quickly resolve a client's presenting problem. Patience is a critical variable in learning to listen before designing an intervention.

As I begin to understand Ruth's experiential world, I have a basis for making interventions. Most of what I will do in my therapeutic work with Ruth is based on the assumption that she can exercise her freedom to change situations, even though the range of this freedom may be restricted by external factors. However, not all of Ruth's problems are internally based, and an exclusive focus on the intrapsychic dimension can lead to blaming her instead of working toward her empowerment.

I assume that Ruth cannot be understood without considering the various systems that affect her—family, social groups, community, church, and other cultural forces. For the counseling process to be effective, it is critical to understand how Ruth influences and is influenced by her social world. (As multicultural, feminist, and family therapists have emphasized, the human condition needs to be understood within the context of a system, which includes the social and cultural framework.) Ignoring either the internal or the external perspectives in understanding Ruth's life experience will restrict my effectiveness with her.

As I work with Ruth, I am not consciously thinking about what set of techniques I am about to use. I adapt the interventions I employ to fit her needs rather than attempting to fit Ruth to my techniques. In deciding on techniques to introduce, I take into account an array of factors about Ruth. I consider her readiness to confront an issue, her cultural background, her value system, and her trust in me. My concern is to help Ruth identify and experience whatever she is feeling, identify ways in which her assumptions influence how she feels and behaves, and experiment with new behaviors.

CONCLUDING COMMENTS

I am convinced that an integrative perspective is needed to effectively counsel the diverse range of clients who seek counseling. Each therapeutic approach has useful dimensions, and accepting the validity of one model does not necessarily imply a rejection of seemingly divergent models. It is not a matter of a theory being "right" or "wrong," for every theory offers a unique contribution to understanding human behavior and has unique implications for counseling practice. Pluralism in society necessitates taking an integrative approach to theory formation.

Of necessity, discussion of the theoretical orientations mention in this chapter has been brief. For a more elaborate discussion of the various theoretical approaches, see *Theory and Practice of Counseling and Psychotherapy* (Corey, 2001c). If you are using the *Student Video and Workbook for the Art of Integrative Counseling* (Corey, 2001a), the first session (The Beginning of Counseling) illustrates some of the principles I've developed in this chapter. Also, Chapter 1 of *Case Approach to Counseling and Psychotherapy* (Corey, 2001b) will provide an overview of the 10 counseling models and will give a comprehensive picture of the case of Ruth, including various practitioners' views regarding Ruth's diagnosis.

2

The Therapeutic Relationship

In my personal approach to counseling, I place central prominence on the client/counselor relationship. The quality of this person-to-person encounter in the therapeutic situation is the stimulus for positive change. My basic attitudes toward the client and my personal characteristics of honesty, integrity, and courage are what I have to offer. Therapy is a journey taken by counselor and client, a journey that delves deeply into the world as perceived and experienced by the client. But this type of quest demands that the therapist also be in contact with his or her own phenomenological world.

DEVELOPING A WORKING RELATIONSHIP

The value of the client/therapist relationship is a common denominator among all approaches, yet some approaches place more emphasis than others do on the role of the relationship. This is especially true of the existential, person-centered, and Gestalt approaches. These relationship-oriented approaches (sometimes known as experiential) are all based on the premise that the quality of the client/therapist relationship is primary, with techniques being secondary. An effective therapeutic relationship fosters a creative spirit of inventing techniques aimed at increasing awareness, which allows clients to change their thinking, feeling, and behaving.

Here are some key notions I find to be central to effective therapy outcomes:

- The quality of the person-to-person encounter in the therapeutic situation is the catalyst for positive change.
- The counselor's chief role is to be present with clients during the therapeutic hour.
- The therapist can best invite clients to grow by modeling authentic behavior.

- The therapist's role is rooted in his or her way of being and attitudes more than in the techniques employed.
- The therapist's attitudes and values are at least as critical as his or her knowledge, theory, or techniques.
- To function optimally, the therapist must have good contact with clients and be centered within him- or herself.
- A therapist who is not sensitively tuned in to his or her own reactions to a client runs the risk of becoming a technician more than an artist.
- Through engagement with clients, the therapist assists clients in developing increased awareness of what they are experiencing in the present.
- The I/Thou relationship enables clients to experience the safety necessary for risk-taking behavior.
- Awareness emerges within the context of a genuine meeting between therapist and client.
- The basic work of therapy is done by the client; the therapist's job is to create a climate in which the client is likely to try out new ways of being.

These somewhat overlapping notions give a sense of the paramount importance of the therapeutic relationship. If you operate in the framework of the relationship-oriented therapies, you will be much less anxious about using the right technique or about stimulating clients to think, feel, or act in a specific manner. Of course, you will most likely utilize a wide range of techniques designed to enhance aspects of the client's experiencing.

As a therapist, you might conceive of your role as a consultant. Your clients tell you what they want and you then serve as a resource person in helping them explore ways in which they have a better chance of getting what they want. As a consultant, you will teach your clients specific strategies they can use in a variety of situations in everyday life.

The kind of person you are and the ways of being you model are the critical factors affecting the client and promoting change. We invite our clients to grow by modeling authentic behavior. The therapist who possesses wide knowledge, both theoretical and practical, yet lacks human qualities of compassion, caring, good faith, honesty, authenticity, and sensitivity, will hardly be able to make a significant difference in the lives of clients.

Self-disclosure is one avenue for letting clients know you and of being real in your work. If you keep yourself hidden during the therapeutic session or if you engage in inauthentic behavior, clients will also remain guarded and persist in their inauthentic ways. Thus, you can help clients become more trusting and open by selectively disclosing your own responses at appropriate times. Of course, this disclosure does not mean an uncensored sharing of every fleeting feeling or thought. Rather, it entails a willingness to share persistent reactions with clients, especially when this sharing is likely to be facilitative. Therapist self-disclosure is a value shared by a number of theoretical orientations including existential therapy, the person-centered approach, Gestalt therapy, reality therapy, and feminist therapy.

The person-centered approach has contributed greatly to an understanding of the central role of the therapeutic relationship in the healing process. Three personal characteristics, or attitudes, of the therapist form the essence of the therapeutic relationship: (1) congruence or genuineness, (2) unconditional positive regard and acceptance, and (3) accurate empathic understanding.

Congruence implies that as a therapist you are real; that is, you are genuine, integrated, and authentic during the therapy hour. You are without a false front, your inner experience and outer expression of that experience match, and you can openly express feelings, thoughts, reactions, and attitudes that are present in the relationship with your client.

In your therapeutic work, a key attitude you need to communicate to your clients is a deep and genuine caring for them personally. This caring is unconditional in that you do not judge clients' feelings, thoughts, and behavior as good or bad. You value and accept clients without placing stipulations on this acceptance. Acceptance recognizes clients' rights to have their own beliefs and feelings.

One of a counselor's main tasks is to understand the client's experience and feelings sensitively and accurately as they are revealed in the moment-to-moment interaction during the therapy session. It is imperative that you strive to sense your client's subjective experience, particularly in the here and now. Empathy requires a deep and subjective understanding of the internal world of the client and a sense of personal identification with the client's experience. By tuning in to your own feelings that are like the client's feelings, you are able to share the client's subjective world. Empathic understanding implies that you will sense your client's feelings *as if* they were your own without becoming lost in those feelings. This empathy on your part deepens the client's self-understanding and helps the client clarify his or her beliefs and worldviews.

Even the action-oriented approaches (such as behavior therapy, cognitive behavioral therapy, rational emotive behavior therapy, and reality therapy) view the quality of the client/therapist relationship as a core element of effective therapy. Practitioners who subscribe mainly to the cognitive behavioral perspectives stress the therapeutic alliance, rapport, and a collaborative working relationship. Unlike a person-centered therapist who is not particularly concerned about techniques, action-oriented therapists view a good working relationship as necessary, but not sufficient, to produce change. Action-oriented therapists use a range of specific interventions to assess and treat clients. Beyond a working relationship, which is monitored throughout the duration of counseling, the cognitive behavioral practitioner is expected to be skilled in tailor making interventions that will help clients change in the direction they choose. A more extensive discussion of the role of techniques as catalysts for assisting clients in changing the ways they are thinking, feeling, and acting is presented in Chapters 6, 7, and 8.

From my perspective, therapy is a deeply *personal* relationship. I am influenced by the existential and person-centered approaches, which emphasize the personal characteristics and attitudes of the therapist. I think the person I am is just as important as my knowledge of counseling theory and the level of my skills. Although it is essential to use techniques effectively—and to have a theoretical base from which to draw a range of techniques—this ability becomes meaningless in the absence of a therapeutic relationship that is characterized by mutual respect and trust.

BECOMING THE CLIENT: Sharing in a Collaborative Partnership

Therapy as a Collaborative Venture

Assume again that you and I are beginning a therapeutic relationship. I want to expand on the idea that therapy is a collaborative effort. I see many advantages to your assuming an active role as a client, meaning that you agree to participate as fully as possible in all phases of assessment and treatment. A number of therapeutic approaches stress this notion of genuine collaboration between client and therapist, including feminist therapists, Adlerians, cognitive behavior therapists, and behavior therapists. Therapy as a collaborative venture involves client and therapist working together toward the same goals. What is meant by a spirit of collaboration, and how can you best be encouraged to assume an active stance in your treatment?

If you appear to be getting little from the therapeutic relationship, I want to examine my part in this outcome by asking myself about my involvement and willingness to risk with you as your therapist. Yet I also explore with you how you might be contributing in part to your lack of progress. I recognize that I cannot make you want to change, yet I can create a climate where together we are able to look at the advantages and disadvantages of making changes. I see the counseling process as a mutual endeavor in which both of us share the responsibility for making change happen, with the final decision resting with you.

The Relationship During the Early Stage of Counseling

During the first few sessions my main task is to assist you in defining and clarifying your problems. My aim is to create a relationship in which you can reveal your story, focus more clearly on what you want to change, and attain a new perspective in dealing with your problems. What do you feel your role should be?

You might be seeking professional assistance because you realize you are not dealing with problem situations satisfactorily. You may seek counseling because you struggle with self-doubt, feel trapped by your fears, or suffer from some form of loss. You may need to heal from psychological wounds. And you might seek help not because you feel plagued by major problems but because you are not coping with daily challenges as effectively as you would like. You may feel caught in a meaningless job, experience frustration because you are not living up to your own goals and ideals, or feel dissatisfied in your interpersonal life. In short, you may be like many people who seek counseling because they realize they are not managing their lives as well as they might. Why have you come for counseling?

CREATING A THERAPEUTIC CLIMATE. Are you willing to engage in self-exploration? The kind of climate I am able to create during the initial sessions is crucial to a good therapeutic relationship. I can make the mistake of working too hard, asking too many questions, or offering quick solutions. If I can create a collaborative partnership with you, I can assist you greatly by teaching you how to assess your own problems and search for your own solutions. How much responsibility are you willing to assume, both inside and outside the sessions? (These aspects are central to both behavior therapy and reality therapy.) You must learn how to identify and clarify problem areas and how to acquire problem-solving skills that you can use in a variety of difficult situations in everyday living. In a sense, from the very first meeting I can be most helpful to you by encouraging you to look within yourself for resources and strengths you can draw on to better manage your life.

CONSIDERING THE CULTURAL CONTEXT. You may feel frustration and anger due to societal factors such as being discriminated against in your workplace because of your age, gender, race, religion, or sexual orientation. It would be a disservice if I encourage you to settle for injustices in an oppressive environment. Instead of merely solving your presenting problem, I can begin supporting you in your efforts to take action within your community to bring about change. To accomplish this, I may need to be prepared to assume a variety of helping roles—educator, advocate, social change agent, and influencer of policy makers.

It is essential that I respect the purpose for which you initiated therapy. If I pay careful attention to what you tell me about what you want, this can be the foundation of our work. My task then becomes encouraging you to weigh the alternatives and to explore the consequences of what you are doing with your life. Even though oppressive forces may be severely limiting the quality of your life, you are not the victim of circumstances beyond your control. What can you do to improve your situation? Together we may be able to discover new courses of action that will lead to a change in your situation.

As I engage you in identifying and assessing your problems, it is essential that I avoid a stance of "blaming the victim." (As both feminist and family systems therapy stress, the source of your problems may be within your environment rather than due to an internal conflict or weakness on your part.) It may be that you come to me not to resolve internal conflicts but to better understand and deal with external stressors in your environment. I am aware that self-reliance and independence may not be a part of your worldview, and interdependence may be a core value in your life. It can be useful to put you in touch with external resources within the community that you can utilize in meeting the demands of daily living. You may need my services and my guidance to be linked to resources within your community. Some of these resources include arranging for legal assistance or assisting you in coping with day-to-day survival issues such as getting a job, arranging for child care, or taking care of an elderly parent.

Treating all clients in the same manner and using the same basic interventions restricts the effectiveness of therapy. The "one size fits all" notion hampers creativity and is likely to result in you feeling misunderstood. What can you tell me about your basic values and beliefs? Understanding your cultural background helps me establish a therapeutic working relationship. Although it is not necessary that I have an in-depth understanding of your culture and worldview, I must know some of your basic beliefs and values if I hope to make significant contact with you. If I am not aware of the central values that guide your behavior and decisions, you will soon pick up on this and will not likely return for further sessions.

UNDERSTANDING THE FAMILY CONTEXT. Individuals are best understood within the context of their relationships and by assessing their interactions within an entire family. I cannot fully understand you by viewing you only from an individual frame of reference. It is necessary to work with you from a person-in-the-environment context, which includes having some appreciation of your family's past and present influence on you. What can you tell me about your family patterns?

From the family systems models, your problems are viewed as an expression of a dysfunction within a family, and these dysfunctional patterns are often thought to be passed across several generations. The one central principle of family systems therapy is that the client is connected to living systems and that change in one part of the system reverberates throughout other parts. Actions by any individual family member will influence all the others in the family, and their reactions will have a reciprocal effect on the individual. Therefore, as your counselor, it is not possible for me to accurately assess your concern without observing the interaction with and mutual influence between the other family members, as well as the broader contexts in which you and your family live. To focus primarily on studying your internal dynamics without adequately considering interpersonal dynamics yields an incomplete picture of you. Your family provides a primary context for understanding how you function in relationship to others and how you behave.

YOUR ROLE AS A COUNSELOR IN CREATING A WORKING RELATIONSHIP

In this section reflect on what attitudes you think would be conducive to establishing good rapport with your clients and think about behavior that you would want to model to your clients.

Establishing the Relationship

If your clients are to feel free to talk about their problems, you need to provide attention, active listening, and empathy. Clients must sense your respect for them, which you can demonstrate by your attitudes and behaviors. You reveal an attitude of respect when you are concerned about your clients' best interests, view them as able to exercise control of their own destiny, and treat them as individuals rather than stereotyping them. You actually show clients that you respect them through your behavior in a session. Some of these behaviors include:

- Actively listening to and understanding clients
- Suspending critical judgment
- Expressing appropriate warmth and acceptance
- Communicating that you understand their world as they experience it
- Providing a combination of support and challenge
- Assisting clients in cultivating their inner resources for change
- Helping clients take the specific steps needed to bring about change

Ask yourself how well you are able to pay attention to others, to fully listen to them, and to empathize with their situation. Assess the qualities you possess that will either help or hinder you in assuming the internal and subjective frame of reference of clients. Consider these questions:

- Do you attend to what clients are telling you both verbally and nonverbally? Do you pay attention mainly to what people tell you with their mouths, or do you also notice the way they deliver their messages?
- Do you let others tell their story, or do you get impatient and want to talk too soon? Do you encourage clients to tell stories in great detail for the sake of your curiosity? Do you have a tendency to get lost in the details of their story and miss the essence of their struggle?
- Do you listen to and detect the core messages when clients speak? How do you check with clients to make certain you are understanding them?
- Do you keep clients focused on issues they want to explore? Do you keep your own centeredness, even when clients may seem very fragmented or are making demands on you?
- Are you able to set aside your own biases for a time and attempt to enter the client's world? For example, if you consider yourself a liberated woman, are you willing to accept the client who tells you she is satisfied in her traditional role as a homemaker?
- Do you communicate your understanding and acceptance to clients?
- Do you work nondefensively with signs of resistance from clients? How do you use this resistance as a way of helping clients explore their issues more deeply?

Although it may seem deceptively simple to merely listen to others, the attempt to understand the world as others see it is demanding. Respect, genuineness, and empathy are best considered "states of being," not mechanical techniques to be used on clients. Establishing a working relationship with clients implies that you are genuine and respectful in behavioral ways, that the relationship is a two-way process, and that the clients' interests assume priority. This means that you avoid doing for clients what they are capable of doing for themselves!

Helping Clients Gain a Focus

People who seek assistance often feel overwhelmed by their problems. By trying to talk about everything that is troubling them in one session, they also may manage to overwhelm you. A focusing process is necessary to provide direction for the therapeutic efforts. To achieve this focus, make an assessment of the major concerns of the client. You could say to a client who presents you with a long list of problems: "We won't be able to deal with all your problems in one session. What was going on in your life when you finally decided to call for help?" Other focusing questions are "At this time in your life, what seems most pressing and troublesome to you?" and "If you could address only one problem today, which one would you pick?"

Once clients determine what concerns they seriously are willing to explore, you can collaborate with them in designing a contract. You can be instrumental in encouraging clients to explore their key issues in terms of their experiences, feelings, and behaviors. By focusing on what is salient in the present, you can assist clients in clarifying their own problems. Dealing with what emerges in the present with your clients provides an excellent direction for you to build further interventions.

Clients may seek you out because they feel that they have lost control of how they are living. They may look to you to direct them, give them advice, and even produce magical cures. But, more than this, they need to be deeply heard and understood. Your trust in them is important in teaching them to trust their own capacity to discover their own unique solutions. Your power to heal others is the result of a process of genuine dialogue with your clients.

MY INTEGRATIVE APPROACH WITH RUTH

See Session 2 (The Therapeutic Relationship) of the *Student Video and Workbook for the Art of Integrative Counseling.*

The Relationship as the Cornerstone of Therapy

I am convinced that one of the most significant factors determining the degree to which Ruth will attain her goals is the therapeutic relationship that she and I create. Counseling is not something that the therapist *does* to a passive client, using skills and techniques. I operate on the premise that Ruth will get the most from her therapy if she knows how the therapeutic process works. I strive to demystify the therapy process by providing information, securing her informed consent, sharing my perceptions of what is going on in the relationship, and by making her an active partner in both assessment and treatment phases. As much as possible, I am concerned with the potentially harmful uses of power dynamics in the relationship with my client. Therefore, I strive to build mutuality and a sense of partnership into the therapeutic endeavor.

Because I trust Ruth to find her own direction in counseling, I will encourage her to participate with me in planning and structuring the sessions. My main focus is on being real, on accepting her feelings and thoughts, on demonstrating my unconditional positive regard for her, and on respecting her as a person. If I am able to listen carefully and reflect what I am hearing, and if I am able to deeply empathize with her life situation, Ruth will be able to clarify her struggles and work out her own solutions to her problems. Although she is only dimly aware of her feelings at the initial phase of therapy, she will move toward increased clarity as I accept her fully, without conditions and without judgments. My main aim is to create a climate of openness, trust, caring, understanding, and acceptance. Then she can use this relationship to move forward and grow.

Our Second Session

I ask Ruth to reflect on any afterthoughts she might have had about our first session. Ruth lets me know that she is not used to looking at herself, nor is she used to being the focus of attention. We'll need to explore this further as much of the therapeutic process deals with clients paying increased attention to what they are experiencing and doing. This gives me an opportunity to introduce the topic of how Ruth can get the most from her therapeutic experience. Together we explore how she can assume an active role by thinking about topics she wants to bring up in her sessions and by deciding on some ways she wants to be different in her daily life. Rather than assuming total responsibility for the direction of Ruth's therapy, I look for ways to collaborate with Ruth on the direction of our work. As a teacher and a consultant, I am helping Ruth learn about the therapy process so that she can eventually continue her own personal growth.

Listening to Ruth's Story

One way of deepening the therapeutic relationship is to demonstrate a genuine interest in the client's story. I began listening to Ruth's self-presentation at the first session, but one meeting is not enough for her to share the many significant turning points in her life. Subsequent sessions are needed for Ruth to flesh out the story of her life. There are a number of ideas I especially like from narrative therapy, which I think has relevance in getting Ruth to tell her story and to begin thinking about the kind of life she would like. Narrative therapy emphasizes the value of devoting time to listening to clients' stories and to looking for past events clients can reinterpret in new ways. Ruth's life story influences what she notices and remembers. In this sense her story influences how she will face the future.

I also make the assumption that many of Ruth's problems have been created by her restricted and self-defeating vision of herself and her world. Part of our work together will be to look for resources within Ruth that will enable her to create a new story for herself. In short, from the narrative perspective my commitment is to help Ruth rewrite the story of her life. Through this collaboration, Ruth can review and reframe certain events from her past and rewrite her future. At this phase of our work I am also influenced by the feminist therapy notion that our collaboration will be aimed at freeing Ruth from the influence of oppressive elements in her social environment and empowering her to become an active agent who is directing her own life.

Although I did not begin the initial session by asking Ruth a series of questions pertaining to her life history, in this session I will ask questions to fill in the gaps in Ruth's story. This method gives a more comprehensive picture of how she views her life now, as well as events that she considers significant in her past. Rather than making it a question-and-answer session, I like the idea of using an *autobiographical approach,* in which Ruth writes about the critical turning points in her life, events from her childhood and adolescent years, relationships with parents and siblings, school experiences, current struggles, and future goals and aspirations.* I ask her what she thinks would be useful for her to recall and focus on and what she imagines would be useful to me in gaining a better picture of her subjective world. In this way Ruth does some reflecting and sorting out of life experiences outside of the session, she takes an active role in deciding what her personal goals will be for therapy, and I have access to rich material that will give me ideas of where and how to proceed with her. This unstructured, or open-ended, autobiography could fit into existential, person-centered, and Gestalt therapy models, in which the emphasis is on the subjective world of the client. Psychoanalytic, Adlerian, and narrative therapists would also want to consider information about her developmental history.

Helping Ruth Externalize Her Problem

Ruth's autobiography provides me with significant clues to the unfolding of the story of her life. Even during the early sessions, I encourage Ruth to separate her *being* from her *problems* by posing questions that *externalize* her problems. Narrative therapy insists that the person is not the problem, and I view Ruth's problems as something separate from her. Ruth presents many problems that are of concern to her, yet we cannot deal with all of

---

* For a list of areas I am likely to explore with Ruth as a way of getting a complete picture, see Corey and Corey's (1997) *I Never Knew I Had a Choice.*

them at once. When I ask her what one problem most concerns her right now, she replies with "Guilt. I feel guilty so often over so many things that I don't do. No matter how hard I work at what is important to me, I generally fall short of what I expect of myself, and then I feel guilty."

From reading Ruth's autobiography and from listening to her story, it becomes clear that her problem-saturated story contains a theme of "guilt." She feels guilty because she is not an adequate daughter, because she is not the mother she thinks she *should* be, and because she is not as accomplished a student as she demands of herself. When Ruth falls short of "perfect performances" in these and other areas, guilt is the result.

My intention is to help Ruth come to view her problem of guilt as being separate from who she is as a person. Toward this end, I ask questions of Ruth about how her guilt occurs and ask her to give examples of situations where she experiences guilt. I am interested in charting the influence of the problem of guilt. Using elements of solution-focused therapy and the narrative approach, I ask Ruth questions aimed at finding exceptions:

- Has there ever been a time when guilt could have taken control of your relationship, but didn't? What was it like for you? How did you do it?
- How is this different from what you would have done before? What does it say about you that you were able to do that?
- How do you imagine your life would be different if you didn't have this problem?
- Can you think of ways that you can begin to take even small steps to divorce yourself from guilt?"

My questioning is aimed at discovering moments when Ruth hasn't been dominated or discouraged by the problem of guilt. This provides a basis for considering how life would be different if guilt were not in control. As our therapy proceeds, I expect that Ruth will gradually come to see that she has more control over her problem of guilt than she believed. As she is able to distance herself from these problematic themes (such as guilt), she will be less burdened by her problem-saturated story and will discover a range of options. She will likely focus more on the resources within herself to construct the kind of life she wants.

CONCLUDING COMMENTS

I want to emphasize that what I consider the single most important element in becoming a competent counselor is your way of being. If you can be fully present and be yourself, you can be a catalyst for clients to engage in introspection, relevant self-disclosure, and risk taking. Knowing who you are is the starting point for developing your own view of counseling. Techniques are always secondary to your personal vitality and your ability to establish and maintain a growth-producing therapeutic relationship.

Techniques are not useful if they are not sensitively adapted to the particular client and context. The outcome of a technique is influenced by the relationship between you and your client. Techniques are merely tools to amplify emerging material that is present and to encourage exploration of issues that have personal relevance to clients. More important than the techniques you use are the attitudes you have toward clients. Your primary function as a therapist is to support clients in their journey of making decisions regarding how they want to live.

After reading this chapter on the therapeutic relationship, take time to reflect on the following questions as a way of clarifying your thoughts on the kinds of relationships you want to create with your clients:

- How do you view the role of techniques in the counseling process?
- What emphasis do you place on the client/therapist relationship? If you had to describe in a few words to your client what you considered a "working relationship" to be, what would you say?
- How important do you consider your self-disclosure to be in your work as a counselor? How can you assess when it might be helpful to your client for you to engage in self-disclosure? What kinds of disclosures are you most likely to make? Are there some disclosures you are not likely to make to clients?
- This chapter emphasizes the notion of therapy as a collaborative venture. To what degree do you agree with this conceptualization of counseling? What are some specific things you are likely to say and do as a counselor during the initial session to establish a collaborative relationship? What are some things you might say to clients about what they can expect of you as their counselor? What would you most expect of them as clients?
- If you were a client in counseling, what kind of relationship would you want and expect from your counselor?

3

Establishing Therapeutic Goals

All theoretical orientations address the central role of goals as a factor in successful outcomes. Although contemporary counseling theories all share *some* goals, there are many differences when it comes to the best route to achieve these goals. Some therapies focus on bringing out feelings, whereas others stress identifying cognitive patterns, and still others concentrate on changes in behavior. This is why I believe a thinking, feeling, and acting approach can be so helpful when integrating theory and technique.

In working with clients you will establish target goals in each of the areas of their functioning. Even with the same client, you will at times be focusing on different dimensions such as changing beliefs or exploring a range of feelings or implementing behavioral changes. It is essential that you be flexible in defining with your clients a variety of goals that provide direction to their therapy. Without clear goals, the counseling sessions will not be productive.

The goals of counseling are almost as diverse as are the theoretical approaches. Goals include restructuring the personality, uncovering the unconscious, creating social interest, finding meaning in life, curing an emotional disturbance, examining old decisions and making new ones, developing trust in oneself, becoming more self-actualizing, reducing anxiety, shedding maladaptive behavior and learning adaptive patterns, gaining more effective control of one's life, becoming aware of and reducing the influence of gender-role socialization, acquiring personal empowerment, and creating new patterns of relationships within a family system. In my own integrative approach there is room to incorporate just about all of these goals. At different stages in therapy, different goals assume prominence. You can work with clients on all levels of human experience by helping them identify a range of specific goals that will provide a framework for the sessions.

The main goal of most theoretical orientations is to bring about changes within an individual in the realms of thinking, feeling, and behaving. These changes, however, often have repercussions on the systems of which the individual is a part. Family systems approaches have a broader goal than merely bringing about change within the individual. In family therapy, and in feminist therapy as well, the goal is to bring about change within systems. When therapy is successful, the family often learns about patterns that have been transmitted from generation to generation or learn ways to detect and solve problems that keep members stuck in dysfunctional relational patterns. Incorporating concepts from systems models into an integrative approach broadens counseling to deal with changing individuals in systems.

BECOMING THE CLIENT: Establishing Counseling Goals

In this section I want to identify basic considerations in the process of formulating meaningful counseling goals. Once again put on your client hat. How can I work with you to identify clear and personal goals to guide the sessions? What are some of the obstacles to formulating concrete goals, and how can we best deal with these obstacles?

To begin with, I have some general goals that are congruent with my philosophy of counseling that will influence the direction of our sessions. One major goal is to establish a therapeutic relationship that will serve as a foundation for all of our work together. Another goal is to operate from a guiding philosophy that will allow for systematic exploration of the personal goals you identify as being important to you as my client. I want to teach you a framework for resolving the problems you bring to counseling, with special emphasis on teaching you how to deal successfully with future problems. What goals do you have for our work together?

Although I have some general goals that are a vital part of the counseling process, it will be up to you to identify personal goals that will determine what we talk about in our sessions. It is likely that you have given a good deal of thought to what you want out of your life, yet you could still benefit from identifying, clarifying, and discovering better ways of reaching your goals. Did you enter our first session with clear, concrete, and realistic goals for the counseling process? It is more likely that you had only a generalized notion of what you wanted to get from your counseling. For example, you might inform me: "I'd just like to feel better about myself. I'm down on myself a lot." It probably would not be of much help to you if I simply asked you to be more concrete. However, a line of self-reflective questions might result in more clarity about what you want for yourself.

- If you were feeling better about yourself, what might you be feeling?
- Assume that you felt better about yourself. What would you be telling me about who you are and how your life is if you felt the way you wanted?
- Can you give me some idea of what goes on in your head when you get down on yourself?

- Tell me about a particular area in your life that you'd like to feel better about. Is there one area that you wished could be different?

By following your lead and gently asking you to say more about specific times that you have felt good or what situations in particular you most struggle with, both you and I will gradually get a sharper picture of what you want. Your goals for counseling will be much more meaningful if you define them for yourself. As I listen to you, my interventions are aimed at getting you to state your goals in such a manner that we both know what you want and have a frame of reference to understand the degree to which you are attaining your goals.

I let you know that determining goals is a joint project. Certainly, I won't be making your decisions about what we'll be exploring during your sessions. I like the Adlerian notion of goal alignment, which means that goal setting involves a mutual, collaborative process. I see it as your responsibility to define the target areas for us to explore in our sessions, yet it is my responsibility to guide you in narrowing down your goals in such a fashion that we will both have a clear picture of how to proceed. Developing goals is not something that you can do at once—simply and quickly. Establishing and refining goals takes time and continued effort, yet doing so will give direction to the counseling process.

The action-oriented therapies (behavior therapy, cognitive behavior therapy, rational emotive behavior therapy, and reality therapy) provide very useful concepts for identifying specific goals at the outset of the therapeutic process. In helping you to achieve your goals, I assume an active and directive role. Although you generally determine *what* behavior will be changed, I typically suggest *how* this behavior can best be modified. In designing a treatment plan, I expect to employ techniques and procedures that are specifically appropriate for your situation. In selecting these strategies, I have a wide range of options. The multimodal approach, which is a form of behavior therapy, provides a context that allows me to borrow techniques from a variety of therapeutic systems and apply them to your unique situation. This approach provides for the therapeutic flexibility and versatility required to effectively achieve a diverse range of goals.

Drawing on the behavioral approaches and reality therapy, you and I identify goals that can be measured or monitored. The goals of reality therapy include behavioral change, better decision making, improving significant relationships, enhanced living, and more effective satisfaction of psychological needs. Can you think of a personal goal that fits one of these categories? These action-oriented therapies provide a specific focus of directional change that allow us to evaluate our work together.

I also ask you to consider long-range goals. What would you most like to be able to say about yourself or your life situation one year from now? Five years from now? The art of developing goals consists of breaking these long-term goals into relatively short-term objectives that lead you in the direction you want to move. The category of goals we might discuss would encompass the full spectrum of your thinking, feeling, and behaving—with a particular focus on specific areas within each of these domains that you most want to change. Together we will continue this process of delineating personal goals by identifying specific steps you are willing to take, both in the session and outside the office, to get what you want from life. Indeed, I expect that your goals will change as counseling progresses. As you learn how best to use the counseling sessions, other concerns will become evident.

Counseling is a collaborative partnership, and I do not accept full responsibility for deciding what the focus of our therapy sessions will be. Rather than working very hard to figure out what you might want, I frequently ask what it is you actually want. Is what you are doing working for you? If not, what are you willing to do to change it? If your current behavior is generally serving you well, you may not feel a strong need to change a particular style. I am likely still to encourage you to look at the price you might be paying for being the way you are, and then the decision whether to change is up to you. It is not my job to decide for you how you should live your life. My job is to help you formulate workable goals and to provide you with the tools you'll need to achieve your goals.

Various Types of Therapeutic Goals

In discussing the matter of values and counseling goals, it is inevitable that you will consider both your personal values and the values you espouse as a counselor. For example, most of you would probably agree that it is good and desirable for clients to strive to know themselves and to make choices about the way they want to live. Many process-oriented goals are part of the therapeutic endeavor, a few of which include clients engaging in self-disclosure, risk-taking, and doing work outside the therapy sessions to bring about change. I articulate these process goals early during the counseling relationship. Not all clients may agree to be guided by the goals and values I deem essential. Some clients may not be interested in becoming their own person but may want to cope better with a particular difficult life situation. To develop an approach to the process of formulating and implementing personal therapeutic goals, examine a wide range of possible cognitive, affective, and behavioral goals as a client.

COGNITIVE GOALS. First, let's examine some possible goals in the cognitive realm that you'd be interested in exploring in your own counseling sessions. My aim is to listen for some of your underlying beliefs, especially thought patterns that seem to present difficulty for you. Since most of you are likely preparing to become counselors, or are already engaged is some type of counseling practice, reflect on these statements to determine the degree to which you hold similar beliefs pertaining to yourself as a counselor in training:

- I must always function competently and perfectly. There is no room for making mistakes, for any mistake means that I'm a failure.
- I really need the continual affirmation of all my clients if I am to feel worthwhile as a professional.

- It is essential that I have the right technique for every problem situation a client presents or else I will surely fall flat on my face and look stupid.
- I am fully responsible for the progress or lack of progress that my clients make.
- If a client does not turn up for a second session, it is most likely due to my ineptness in making good contact with this person at the first meeting.

In listening to self-statements such as these I strive to zero in on core beliefs that potentially result in problematic emotional and behavioral consequences. For instance, are you convinced that you are completely responsible for your clients' therapeutic outcomes? Your core beliefs have a number of consequences. You probably worry excessively about your clients and experience a great deal of stress in your work. Not only does the belief that you are totally responsible for client outcomes cause you anxiety, this belief actually contributes to client dependency.

AFFECTIVE GOALS. As my client, I ask you about the realm of emotions you are experiencing, especially feelings that you view as problematic. I tend to notice any bodily changes that may indicate emergent feelings. Rather than interpret what you are feeling, my tendency is to ask you. As you are talking, what did you just become aware of? I notice that you just teared up. Are you aware of that? What are you experiencing right now? I find that it is most useful to begin work with the affective realm and then move to an exploration of thoughts and behaviors.

I invite you to be as specific as possible in identifying emotional concerns. You might say that you are frightened of intimacy. First of all, it would be important for me to know if this is a situation that you want to change. You may shy away from getting too close to people because of a host of fears, yet keeping distant could well be acceptable to you. It is not my job to urge you to take risks in this area if you do not want to be different. However, if you'd like to be able to experience closeness with a few people and not flee from intimacy, this could become a target goal for our work.

I tend to draw heavily from Gestalt therapy as an effective way to assist you in getting closer to your moment-by-moment experiencing. By asking you to notice what you are aware of in the present moment, you are better able to move into whatever realm is salient for you—be it awareness of a thought, a bodily state, or feelings. If it is appropriate, we might use a range of experiential techniques to deal with affective goals that are important to you.

BEHAVIORAL GOALS. In addition to setting cognitive and affective goals, it is essential that we identify behavioral goals. We might explore your self-defeating thinking patterns, and you might express a range of feelings in sessions, yet therapy can hardly be complete without establishing concrete behavioral goals. Let's assume that you let me know that you would like to take better care of yourself. You realize that too often you feel you are being driven, rather than doing the driving. You contribute to this sense of constant pressure by telling yourself that you don't have time to take care of yourself. Using elements of behavior therapy, reality therapy, and rational emotive behavior therapy, I invite you to examine the choices you are making about your body and your overall wellness. I ask you to examine your present level of physical and psychological well-being. What balance do you want to achieve in areas such as rest, exercise, diet, and ways you spend time? Ask yourself which of these behavioral goals might fit for you as a client.

- I am willing to keep a record of what I do in my work to determine whether there are some patterns that I want to change.
- I am willing to make more time for rest and sleep.
- I want to create a better balance between work and leisure.
- I am willing to ask for help when I feel overwhelmed.
- I want to decide on what kind of exercise program I would most profit from and enjoy.
- I am interested in improving my diet. I am willing to start by monitoring what and how much I eat and drink to determine if there are areas I want to change.

Identifying counseling goals may seem like a simple matter, but counseling is not a linear process of resolving a single problem. You are a complex and integrated being, and any one problem you have is best seen as one aspect of the larger picture. Counseling is more complex and interesting than simply resolving problems.*

GOAL-DIRECTED BEHAVIOR AND GOAL SETTING

I find the Adlerian approach particularly valuable in establishing therapeutic goals. Several key Adlerian concepts have special relevance for the process of establishing goals, both for therapy and for life: the goal-directedness of behavior, struggling with feelings of inferiority, striving for superiority, and social interest. Alfred Adler's system emphasizes the social determinants of behavior. This "socioteleological" approach implies that we are primarily motivated by social forces and strive to achieve certain goals. Adler's view is that we create both short- and long-term goals that motivate our behavior and influence our personality development. It is our long-term goals in particular that guide our movement toward an envisioned completion and sometimes even toward perfection.

* For a further discussion of the goals of counseling and psychotherapy, see Welch and Gonzalez (1999; Chapter 1).

Another key concept from the Adlerian approach that is directly related to the process of forming goals is the notion of social interest. This concept embodies the feeling of being connected to all of humanity—past, present, and future—and to being involved in making the world a better place. Social interest is the individual's positive attitude toward other people in the world that involves a sense of identification and empathy with others. As an antidote to social isolation and self-absorption, social interest leads to courage, optimism, and a true sense of belonging. Our happiness and success are largely related to social connectedness. As social beings we have a need to be of use to others and to establish meaningful relationships in a community. We cannot be understood in isolation from our social context. We are primarily motivated by a desire to belong. Only within the group can we actualize our potential.

CLARIFYING COUNSELING GOALS WITH RUTH

See Session 3 (Establishing Therapeutic Goals) of the *Student Video and Workbook for the Art of Integrative Counseling.*

During the beginning stages, I assist Ruth in getting a clearer grasp of what she most wants from therapy as well as seeing some steps she can begin to take to attain her objectives. Like most clients Ruth is rather global in stating her goals in her autobiography, so I work with her on becoming more concrete. When she looks in the mirror, Ruth says she does not like what she sees. She would like to have a better self-image and be more confident. In general she says that she is dissatisfied with her body. I am interested in knowing specifically what she does not like, the ways in which she now lacks confidence, and what it feels like for her to confront herself by looking at herself and talking to me about what she sees.

Ruth reports that she would like to be more assertive. When she says this, I help her pinpoint specific instances in which she is not assertive and ask her to describe what she actually does or does not do in such circumstances. We consistently move from general to specific. The more concrete she is, the greater are her chances of attaining what she wants. It is from behavior therapy that I have learned the value of specifying goals.

I suggest that Ruth use a journal to keep track of how she is doing in meeting her goals. Journal writing can bring a clarity to Ruth's work in the therapy sessions, and this practice is a good way to extend the influence of what we do together into her daily life. If Ruth experiences difficulties in applying what she is learning in therapy to daily life, writing about it will be an excellent way to figure out alternative strategies. She can bring to her sessions the essence of some of what she writes in her journal.

It is essential that Ruth give considerable thought to what she wants to explore in the counseling sessions. I want to convey to Ruth that she is the one who must come up with her own goals—not goals that she thinks others want for her and certainly not goals that I aspire to for her. Ruth must decide what she wants to explore and the areas she is most interested in changing. Ruth will be able to make progress toward her self-defined goals because she is willing to become actively involved in challenging her assumptions and in carrying out behavioral exercises, both in the sessions and in her daily life. For instance, Ruth establishes a number of goals that she is interested in pursuing in the counseling sessions. She does not like her appearance, she is experiencing considerable difficulty with her daughter (Jennifer), and she would like to improve her relationship with her husband. In a later session, Ruth decides that she wants to enroll in a fitness class as part of her exercise program. The class is full, however, which gives Ruth an opportunity to practice her assertive behavior skills. She is successful and is able to attend the class. Previously it would not even have occurred to Ruth to seek out the instructor and ask to be admitted to a class that was already full. Ruth learns early on the importance of making specific plans aimed at translating what she is learning in the therapy sessions to various segments in her daily life. Although my job is to help Ruth learn how to change, she is the one who actually chooses to apply these skills, making change possible.

In the process of assisting Ruth in identifying personal goals, I borrow from reality therapy by asking her to look at the direction of her life. What is her life like at this time? What seems to be working for her? What feelings, thoughts, and actions are not moving her in the direction she would like to evolve? I might well ask Ruth to project her life one year hence and describe what she would like to say that she has become or achieved. My aim in doing this is to invite Ruth to evaluate what she is presently doing to determine if her actions are getting her what she wants. To help Ruth pinpoint what she wants, I ask her these questions:

- If you were the person that you wish you were, what kind of person would you be?
- What would you be doing if you were living as you would want?
- Is what you are doing at this time taking you closer or farther away from your main goals?

This line of questioning will focus Ruth on the process of critically thinking about where she is now and where she would like to go in the immediate future. This kind of self-evaluation is at the heart of reality therapy.

One of the aspects of reality therapy that I especially value is the emphasis placed on guiding clients in the self-evaluation process. If I have an agenda for Ruth, rather than helping her create her own agenda, then counseling is likely to fail. However, by consistently expecting Ruth to engage in a self-evaluation process she will conduct an inner inventory of her own actions, cognitions, and feelings. Once Ruth decides for herself that her present behavior is not working, she will be much more open to participating collaboratively in designing goals that will meet her needs. Once clear goals are established in a collaborative fashion, meaningful evaluation of the progress of therapy can be charted. At each session, it will be critical that Ruth and I spend a brief amount of time assessing the degree to which counseling is helping her attain her goals. If her goals seem to lose vitality, this is a sign that we need to take another look at the priority topics for our sessions.

At the beginning of most sessions Ruth and I will discuss at least briefly what she wants from this particular session. Questions I tend to ask are: What are you aware of as you approach this session? How do you want to use your time in here today? What is it that you want to talk about? What are you hesitating to explore, yet think it would be important for you to talk about? With these focusing questions, the responsibility is with Ruth to determine what her therapy goals are for each session. In short, I see goal setting as an ongoing process that is best defined *with* the client. It is my job to teach her how to become a collaborator in selecting both short- and long-term goals as well as being a partner in deciding how she wants to use her therapy hour.*

CONCLUDING COMMENTS

It is essential to be flexible in defining with your client a variety of goals that provide direction to therapy. Without clear goals, it is a sure bet that the counseling sessions will not be productive. Carefully consider the purposes for which your clients seek counseling and then collaboratively design specific, clear, and realistic goals to guide the therapeutic process. In reflecting on the construction of your own integrative approach to counseling, be sure to develop a systematic way of incorporating cognitive, affective, and behavioral goals as a starting point for therapy.

---

* For a further discussion of counseling goals with Ruth, see the different practitioners' perspectives presented in Chapters 2 through 11 of *Case Approach to Counseling and Psychotherapy* (Corey, 2001b).

4 Understanding and Dealing With Diversity

In this chapter I will examine the role of diversity in an integrative counseling model. There are many types of diversity to consider, but perhaps the ones that come to mind most readily revolve around race and ethnicity. I would like to broaden this discussion to include spirituality as well as cultural factors. As you read, think about how open you are to learning about diversity as it pertains to your counseling practice. What will it take for you to become multiculturally competent? What part will spirituality play in your counseling style?

MULTICULTURAL CONCERNS

Multiculturalism is a reality that cannot be ignored by practitioners if they hope to meet the needs of their increasingly diverse client groups. Although there is a growing movement toward creating a separate multicultural theory of counseling and therapy (Sue, Ivey, & Pedersen, 1996), I am convinced that current theories can be expanded to incorporate a multicultural component. Many of the key concepts of these theories can be adapted to a cultural framework that has meaning for diverse client groups.

But let me add a caution about generalizing to a particular racial, ethnic, or cultural group. Individuals within a particular group may differ more than individuals from various groups. I like the perspective taken by Vontress, Johnson, and Epp (1999), who advocate a conceptual approach to counseling in which the focus is always on the individual rather than on the individual's race, ethnicity, or cultural background. Despite cultural differences, they maintain that it is important to recognize that people are more alike than different. They remind us that clients often seek counseling over problems in living that do not pertain primarily to their race, ethnicity, or culture of origin.

Vontress and his colleagues place emphasis on basic human conditions that transcend culture, such as existential concerns about living, loving, and dying. Being existentially oriented, these writers state that a human-to-human encounter is therapeutic for all clients, regardless of their cultural background. In short, mental health problems are best understood in a cultural context, but it is essential to remember that each client is a unique individual. The central challenge you will face working with clients who differ from you is to find a way to pay attention to what is significant to them and to get into their world. You can accomplish this goal by listening to what your client is expressing and respecting what you hear.

VARIOUS PERSPECTIVES ON DIVERSITY

In the multicultural field there are two approaches to understanding and working with the diverse worldviews of client populations. One approach is the universal, or transcultural, perspective, which is grounded on the premise that basic human dimensions are important regardless of culture (Fukuyama, 1990). The universal approach to multicultural counseling explores the commonalities of the experiences of people of color. This approach proposes transcultural models as a way to train multiculturally effective counselors. According to Fukuyama (1990), overemphasis on the differences that separate one cultural group from another may promote stereotyping. Fukuyama proposes training programs that include these topics:

- Understanding the concept of culture as a whole as it affects the individual, society, and the therapeutic process
- Providing a broad view of culture that encompasses gender, sexual orientation, age, ethnicity, and race
- Providing information on all forms of oppression including racism, sexism, ageism, and homophobia
- Exploring the importance of gender roles
- Facilitating the individual's identity development as a member of a specific culture
- Facilitating an understanding of one's own worldview and how it relates to family and one's cultural background
- Encouraging loyalty and pride in one's own culture and family ties

In contrast, the focused approach argues for the necessity of gaining in-depth knowledge of specific cultures (Locke, 1990). Locke argues for a provincial perspective as a requisite for an adequate philosophy of multicultural counseling. In his challenge of the universal approach, Locke asserts that counselors need to gain cultural expertise about specific culturally different individuals or groups that they are likely to encounter in their practice.

Paul Pedersen espouses a viewpoint on multicultural counseling that encompasses aspects of both Fukuyama's (1990) universal approach and Locke's (1990) provincial approach. According to Pedersen (1997), the multicultural perspective seeks to provide a conceptual framework that both recognizes the complex diversity of a pluralistic society and suggests bridges of shared concern that link all people, regardless of their differences. This perspective looks both at the unique dimensions of a person and at how this person shares themes with those who are different. Such a perspective respects the needs and strengths of diverse client populations, and it recognizes the experiences of these clients. Mere knowledge of certain cultural groups is not enough; it is important to understand the variability within groups. Each individual must be seen against the backdrop of his or her cultural group, the degree to which he or she has become acculturated, and the level of development of racial identity.

Pedersen (1997, 2000) emphasizes the importance of understanding both group and individual differences in making accurate interpretations of behavior. Whether practitioners pay attention to cultural variables or ignore them, culture will continue to influence both the client's and the therapist's behavior, and the counseling process as well. Counselors who ignore culture will provide less effective services.

Pedersen (cited in Nystul, 1999b) has moved toward a culture-centered approach to counseling, maintaining that accurate assessment, meaningful understanding, and effective intervention demand that the client's cultural context be *central* to the counseling process. Pedersen defines culture broadly to include ethnographic, demographic, status, and affiliation variables. Using this framework, all counseling can be considered multicultural. He contends that by defining culture broadly it is possible to view culture as the "thousand persons" we all have collected from various sources who follow us wherever we go and who influence all our decisions. For us to have a sense of cultural self-awareness, it is necessary for us to have access to and dialogue with those inner voices.

Technical eclecticism seems especially necessary in working with a diverse range of cultural backgrounds. Harm can come to clients who are expected to fit all the specifications of a given theory, whether or not the values espoused by the theory are consistent with their own cultural values. As counselors, it is important to keep in mind that rather than stretching your client to fit the dimensions of a single theory you must make your theory and practice fit the unique needs of the client. This requirement calls for you to possess knowledge of various cultures, awareness of your own cultural heritage, and skills to assist diverse clients in meeting their needs within the realities of their culture.

Counselors must be able to assess the special needs of clients. Depending on the individual client's ethnicity and culture and also on the concerns that bring this person to counseling, you will need to show flexibility in utilizing diverse therapeutic strategies. Some clients will need more direction and guidance; others will be very hesitant in talking about themselves in personal ways, especially early in the counseling process. What may appear to be resistance is very likely to be the client's response to years of cultural conditioning and respect for certain values and traditions. It is important to be familiar with a variety of theoretical approaches and have the ability to employ and adapt your techniques to fit the person-in-the-environment. It is not enough to merely assist clients in gaining insight, expressing suppressed emotions, or making certain behavioral changes. The challenge you face is to find practical strategies for adapting the techniques you have developed to enable clients to question the impact their culture continues to have on their lives. They are then able to make decisions about what facets of their existence they want to keep and what they would like to change.

Being an effective counselor involves reflecting on how your own culture influences you and your interventions in your counseling practice. This awareness will be a critical factor in your becoming more sensitive to the cultural backgrounds of the clients who seek your help. An integrative perspective favors broadening the base of contemporary theories to encompass a social, spiritual, and even political dimension.*

THEORIES APPLIED TO DIVERSITY PERSPECTIVES

In this section I summarize briefly some of the various theoretical systems from the vantage point of their contributions to understanding diversity. I have included key concepts that I find most useful in understanding and working with clients from a multicultural perspective. Each of these main points is an element that I include in my integrative approach to counseling practice.

Adlerian Contribution to Diversity

The Adlerians' focus on social interest, on belonging, and on the collective spirit fits well with the value systems of many diverse client populations. Cultures that stress the welfare of the social group and that emphasize the role of the family will find the Adlerian focus on social interest to be congruent with their values. Not only is Adlerian theory congruent with the values of many cultural groups, but the approach offers flexibility in applying a range of cognitive and action-oriented techniques to help clients explore their practical problems.

If culture is defined broadly to include age, roles, sexual orientation, and gender differences, there can be cultural differences even within a family. The Adlerian approach emphasizes the value of subjectively understanding the unique world of the individual. Culture is one significant dimension for grasping the subjective and experiential perspective of an individual.

---

* For further discussion of these topics, I highly recommend Sue and Sue (1999), *Counseling the Culturally Different: Theory and Practice* (3rd ed.); Vontress, Johnson, and Epp (1999), *Cross-Cultural Counseling: A Casebook;* and Pedersen (2000), *A Handbook for Developing Multicultural Counseling Awareness.*

Existential Contribution to Diversity

Because it is grounded in the universal characteristics of human beings, Vontress, Johnson, and Epp (1999) contend that the existential approach is perhaps the most applicable of all approaches for working with culturally diverse clients. Of all the counseling theories, the existential approach comes closest to describing the universal human experiences that transcend the boundaries that separate cultures.

Vontress and his colleagues indicate that we are all multicultural in the sense that we are the product of many cultures. Vontress and his colleagues encourage counselors in training to focus on the universal commonalities of clients first and secondarily on areas of differences.

Gestalt Therapy's Contribution to Diversity

There are many opportunities to apply Gestalt experiments in creative ways with diverse client populations. Gestalt experiments can be tailored to fit the unique way in which an individual perceives and interprets his or her culture. Gestalt therapists approach each client in an open way and without preconceptions. This is essential in working with clients from other cultures. Moreover, Gestalt therapists attempt to fully understand the background of their clients' culture. They are concerned about how and which aspects of this background become central or figural for them and what meaning clients place on these figures.

Reality Therapy's Contribution to Diversity

Many of the key concepts of reality therapy can easily be applied when working with a diverse range of clients. I especially value the straightforward approach of asking clients to look at what they are doing to determine the degree to which their actions are satisfactory to them. Once clients decide what thoughts, feelings, and behaviors they want to target for change, I employ reality therapy procedures in designing action plans to bring about these changes.

Wubbolding (2000) believes reality therapy needs to be modified to fit the cultural context of people other than North Americans. Wubbolding has found that some of the direct questions and confrontations that he uses with Western clients must be adapted with non-Western clients. He points to some basic language differences between Japanese and Western cultures. North Americans are inclined to say what they mean, to be assertive, and to be clear and direct in asking for what they want. In Japanese culture, assertive language is not appropriate, and communication is less direct. The reality therapist's tendency to ask direct questions may need to be softened, with questions being raised more elaborately and indirectly. It may be a mistake, for example, to ask individualistic questions built around whether specific behaviors meet clients' needs. Flexibility in using techniques is a foremost requirement in working with culturally diverse clients, and key concepts and procedures must be tailored to fit specific client populations.

Cognitive Behavioral Contribution to Diversity

The cognitive behavioral approaches have certain advantages in multicultural counseling situations. For some clients, the free expression of feelings and sharing personal concerns may be inhibited. A cognitive behavioral orientation places emphasis on therapists functioning as teachers who encourage clients to learn skills to deal with the problems of living. From this orientation, the stress is on changing specific behaviors and developing problem-solving skills rather than expressing feelings. Clients who are looking for action plans and behavioral change will be receptive to this therapy because it offers concrete methods for dealing with their problems.

One aspect of the cognitive behavioral approaches that I especially appreciate is providing clients with a framework to think about their thinking. Within the framework of their cultural values and worldview, clients can explore their beliefs and provide their own reinterpretations of significant life events. This allows therapists to guide clients in a manner that respects clients' underlying values. This dimension is especially important when counselors do not share the same worldview and cultural background as their clients.

Feminist Contribution to Diversity

Feminist therapy and multicultural perspectives of therapy practice have a great deal in common. Feminist therapy demands recognition of the role oppressive environmental forces have played in keeping women subjugated to men. The feminist perspective of understanding the use of power in relationships has application for understanding power inequities due to racial and cultural factors as well. Neither feminist nor multicultural therapists are willing to settle for adjustment to the status quo. Nor does either approach rest solely on individual change; both demand direct action for social change as part of the role of therapists. Many of the social action and political strategies that call attention to oppressed groups have equal relevance for women and for ethnic minorities. Therapists who subscribe to the assumptions underlying feminist and multicultural perspectives demonstrate their belief that therapy should free individuals and increase their range of choices.

RECOGNIZING THE SPIRITUAL DOMAIN

Spirituality, like the cultural dimension, might very well be at the center of an integrative approach. Clients' spiritual values should be viewed as a potential resource in therapy rather than as something to be ignored. Research has indicated that counselors' values influence every phase of the therapeutic process, including the theories of personality and therapeutic change, assessment strategies, therapy goals, and the selection of intervention strategies (Richards, Rector, & Tjeltveit, 1999). There is growing empirical evidence that our spiritual values and behaviors can promote physical and psychological well-being (Richards & Bergin, 1997; Richards, Rector, & Tjeltveit, 1999).

Spirituality and religion have been the subject of increasing debate in recent years, and there is now widespread interest in the spiritual and religious beliefs of both counselors and clients and how much beliefs might be incorporated in therapeutic relationships (see Miller, 1999b). Publications of the American Counseling Association (ACA) and the American Psychological Association (APA) are signs that these key professional organizations recognize the importance of spiritual issues in counseling practice. Survey data of both practicing counselors and counselor educators indicate that spiritual and religious matters are therapeutically relevant, ethically appropriate, and potentially significant topics for the practice of counseling in secular settings (Burke et al., 1999).*

Assessing Your Own Spirituality

Your own value system influences every facet of your counseling practice, including your assessment strategies, your views of goals of treatment, the interventions used, the topics explored during the sessions, and evaluations of therapy outcomes. Indeed, no therapy is value-free. You have an ethical responsibility to be aware of how your beliefs affect your work and make sure you do not unduly influence your clients. Take a moment to reflect on these questions:

- What role does spirituality or religion play in your life?
- Does religion or spirituality provide you with a source of meaning?
- What connection, if any, do you see between spirituality and religion?
- What are your views concerning established, organized religions?
- Has religion been a positive, negative, or neutral force in your life?
- How do you think your views on spirituality and religion influence your perspective on the counseling process?

Even if spiritual and religious issues are not the focus of a client's concern, these values may enter into the sessions indirectly as your client explores moral conflicts or grapples with questions of meaning in life. Can you maintain objectivity when spiritual and religious values are explored

---

* In recognition of this the ACA has published Burke and Miranti (1992, 1995), Kelly (1995), and Hinterkopf (1998). Recent publications of the APA include Miller (1999b), Richards and Bergin (1997), and Shafranske (1996). I recommend all of these readings in the area of the place of spirituality in counseling.

in counseling sessions? How do you think your values will influence the way you counsel? If you have little belief in spirituality or are hostile to organized religions, can you empathize with clients who view themselves as being deeply spiritual or who feel committed to the teachings of a particular church? If you are convinced that having a meaning in life hinges on accepting certain religious beliefs, can you be of help to clients who do not share your conviction?

Acknowledging Clients' Spirituality

Spirituality and religion are critical sources of strength for many clients and are the bedrock for finding meaning in life. Some clients cannot be understood without appreciating the central role of religious or spiritual beliefs and practices. Spirituality is a significant aspect of well-being and can be instrumental in promoting healing. To ignore the spiritual side of individuals could be a serious mistake.

Counselors ask just about every imaginable question about a client's life, yet they sometimes do not inquire about the meaning of spirituality and religion. An integrative perspective allows for the assessment of spiritual values and practices. If counselors do not raise the issue of how spirituality is viewed by their clients, clients might well assume that counseling ought to be divorced from any discussion of religion and spirituality.

Certainly it is unethical to attempt to convert clients to a particular religious or spiritual set of values. But you can assist clients in exploring their own values to determine the degree to which they are living within the framework of this value system. My hope is that you will monitor yourself for subtle ways you might be inclined to push certain values in your counseling practice, either toward embracing a particular spiritual perspective or abandoning such values. It is critical to keep in mind that it is the client's role to determine what specific values to retain or modify.

The Place of Spirituality in Assessment and Treatment

As a counselor, you will be challenged to address spiritual and religious beliefs in both assessment and treatment practices, *if these beliefs are important to the client.* Bergin (1991) and many other researchers believe discussing spiritual and religious values will result in a change in the focus of treatment away from symptom relief and toward more general changes in lifestyle. Spirituality is an important component of mental health, and its inclusion in psychotherapy practice renders the treatment process more effective.*

---

* Spiritual and religious values can be integrated into the therapy process using a variety of methods and through a number of different theoretical orientations. Several writers recommend techniques for working with values that should be part of a multidimensional, integrative approach to counseling practice. See Richards and Bergin (1997), Richards, Rector, and Tjeltveit (1999), and Hinterkopf (1998).

Spiritual and religious beliefs can be used to the client's benefit to enhance the therapeutic process. In writing about spirituality and health, Miller and Thoresen (1999) remind us that spiritual and religious involvement is central in many clients' lives and is frequently associated with positive health outcomes. Both religion and counseling help people ponder questions of "Who am I?" and "What is the meaning of my life?" At their best, both counseling and religion foster healing through an exploration of self. Some of the ways spirituality can influence successful treatment outcomes include learning to accept oneself, forgiving others and oneself, admitting one's shortcomings, accepting personal responsibility, letting go of hurts and resentments, dealing with guilt, and learning to let go of self-destructive patterns of thinking, feeling, and acting. To be able to address these values with clients without imposing your spiritual views is certainly part of ethical and effective practice.

UNDERSTANDING RUTH FROM A DIVERSITY PERSPECTIVE

See Session 4 (Understanding and Dealing With Diversity) of the *Student Video and Workbook for the Art of Integrative Counseling.*

Ruth brings up the point that she and I are different. When I inquire about *how* we are different and what this means to her, Ruth mentions the fact that she is a woman and I am a man and implies that we have experienced a different type of socialization. As I mentioned earlier, certain differences between client and counselor cannot be ignored. Yet more important than the specific ways that Ruth and I differ is the matter of which differences are salient for Ruth. I cannot assume that I automatically know the meaning of our differences, even if they seem obvious. I ask Ruth what differences particularly stand out to her and what meaning these differences hold for her. My aim is to make it easier for Ruth to talk about whatever differences she is aware of and how these differences affect her in our relationship.

Ruth does wonder if I can really empathize with her experience as a woman. In many ways Ruth has been socialized to obediently follow traditional roles and behave in ways that others expect of her. Although she does not identify herself as being an oppressed person, she does seem to be oppressed in some respects. Because of our differences in gender and socialization, Ruth wonders if we can work together. I let Ruth know that it might be difficult for me to understand some aspects of her life, and also let her know that I will tell her when I am having trouble grasping her subjective perspective. For instance, it may be challenging for me to understand the power of the socialization she has experienced and how difficult it is for her to change certain roles that she has been playing for most of her life. I also invite her to tell me whenever she feels that our differences are getting in her way. I do not want to make certain prior assumptions about my ability to work effectively with Ruth until we have had an opportunity to work together for at least a short time.

Principles of feminist therapy can provide useful guidelines in understanding the therapeutic implications of ways that Ruth and I have unique life experiences. I can provide a context for Ruth to evaluate how oppression may be operating in her life today. As a woman, she has learned to put her personal needs on the back burner and to focus on her role as caretaker for her family. This makes it difficult for Ruth to identify and honor what she wants out of therapy. I need to monitor my own perceptions, which are filtered through the lens of my experiences and which may not be the same as Ruth's. Because oppression profoundly influences Ruth's beliefs, choices, and perceptions, we will examine the cultural context of how her gender-role socialization is influencing her behavior now.

RUTH BRINGS UP HER SPIRITUALITY. Although I do not have an agenda to impose religious or spiritual values on Ruth, I do see it as my function to assess the role spirituality plays in her life currently—and to assess beliefs, attitudes, and practices from her earlier years. Ruth grew up attending a fundamentalist religious group, and she very much hopes I will be able to understand this aspect of her upbringing. Several times Ruth initiated a discussion about the void she feels in the area of religion. When she does bring up this topic, I certainly want to honor her request to seriously consider the personal meaning religious themes have for her.

Ruth was taught that she should never question the religious and moral values that were "right." Eventually Ruth rejected much of the guilt-oriented aspects of her religion, but on an emotional level she still felt a sense of unease and has yet to find what she considers a viable alternative to the religion of her parents. At this time I do not have a vested interest in having Ruth return to her former beliefs or to find a new religion to replace the one she rejected. I want to pay attention to where Ruth appears to be stuck, or where she is conflicted, or what she most hopes she could change as it pertains to religion.

Ruth lets me know that mainly what she remembers from her church experiences is feeling a sense of guilt that she was not good enough and that she always fell short of being the person her church and parents thought she should be. Not only was she not enough in the eyes of her parents, but she was also not enough for God. With this disclosure my aim would be to discuss the guilt Ruth experiences. Guilt is a natural response when we fail to meet our own standards or when we are not living in accordance with our core values. However, guilt that results in self-criticism and self-condemnation is hardly healthy. I would work with Ruth to reframe the role guilt serves in her life.

Ruth is engaged in a struggle to find spiritual values that will help her find meaning in her life. Although formal religion does not seem to play a key role for Ruth now, she is struggling to find her place in the universe. Ruth is seeking spiritual avenues that provide her with purpose, but she is floundering somewhat and realizes that this is a missing dimension in her life. I see my role as encouraging her to remain open to pursuing a variety of spiritual pathways that may make sense to her.

Ruth lets me know that she is pleasantly surprised that I am even mentioning religion and spirituality. She was not sure whether it was appropriate to bring such matters into counseling. She lets me know that it was good for her to be able to initiate a discussion about her past experiences with religion and her present quest to find a spiritual path that has meaning to her. Ruth informs me of her intention to further explore in her sessions ways that she can enhance her spiritual life. I will remain open to these discussions as they are introduced by Ruth.

CONCLUDING COMMENTS

Diversity is a reality that must be factored into an integrative approach to counseling. Regardless of theoretical orientation, both clients' and therapists' underlying values need to be taken into account. Some of the values implicit in contemporary counseling theories include an emphasis on individualism, the separate existence of the self, and individuation as the foundation for maturity. But these values may not be equally relevant to all people, and therapists must recognize that contemporary counseling theories are not value-neutral.

The psychoanalytic, behavioral, cognitive behavioral, and existential approaches originated in the Euro-American culture and are grounded on a core set of values. There is a danger of imposing these values as being the only right ones and as having universal applicability. The relationship-oriented therapies—such as person-centered theory, existential therapy, and Gestalt therapy—emphasize freedom of choice and self-actualization. If you base your practice on these orientations, you will likely focus on individual responsibility for making internal changes as a way to cope with problems, and you will view individuation as the foundation for healthy functioning. Listen to your clients and determine why they are seeking help and how best to deliver the help that is appropriate for them in their unique context.

5

Understanding and Dealing With Resistance

As a trainee in counseling, one of your biggest fears might be getting stuck with a highly resistant client. If you are like many beginning counselors, you take resistance in those with whom you are working in personal ways. You might tell yourself: "If I were an effective counselor, I shouldn't have a resistant client. I should be able to help just about anybody who comes to me. If clients get stuck, or are uncooperative, or don't come back for a second session, this is a sure sign of my inadequacy as a counselor. Maybe I should get into another line of work—quick!"

Your self-talk may not be quite so harsh, yet faced with client resistance you might well blame yourself for what you've done or failed to do. In any event, I doubt that you would actually welcome resistance as the source of productive material for therapeutic work. Take a few moments to think about the meanings you attach to resistance. Is it a part of every counseling venture, regardless of how motivated the client is and how skillful the counselor is? Is resistance a client's plot to sabotage your best efforts? Just what is resistance?

One of my colleagues has trouble with the word "resistance," thinking of it as a negative term that implies something is wrong with the client. She does have a good point, since resistance often is equated with stubborn refusal to cooperate with treatment, is viewed as something the client is doing wrong, or is perceived by counselors as a sign of their ineptness. However, my view of resistance is that it is a normal phenomenon that is basic to the counseling process. Resistance is a fundamental part of therapy that must be recognized and explored. I agree with the psychoanalytic conceptualization of resistance as defensive strategies aimed at preserving one's inner core in the face of anxiety. Once resistance is identified, it can be addressed cognitively, affectively, and behaviorally in an integrative way.

From a behavioral perspective I am reminded that what I identify as "resistance" might well be an excuse on my part for not doing a thorough assessment or for inadequately utilizing techniques. This perspective requires that I look at what I am doing to determine how I might be getting in my client's way. Chapter 3 emphasized the value of the therapist working with clients to establish clear and realistic personal goals as a framework for the direction of counseling. If I impose my vision of what I think the client should be working on, resistance is to be expected.

Resistance is too often viewed as an impediment to therapeutic progress when, in actuality, it is central to productive work. I agree with Preston (1998) that for most clients resistances are not impediments to therapy—they *are* the therapy. He views the challenge to therapists as learning how to manage resistances, not to eliminate them. Preston believes much of therapy involves removing roadblocks, freeing up and expanding internal experiencing, and eventually stepping back and watching clients move along the pathway of healing. As I hope to illustrate, by coming to understand and deal with your own patterns of resistance, you open up possibilities for modifying your behavior and also for developing skills in managing resistance in clients.

In understanding the dynamics of resistance, both clients' and therapists' contributions to the resistance must be considered. Certainly, I don't want clients to feel blamed or to come to the conclusion that something is inherently wrong with them for experiencing resistance. However, I don't think resistance always implies a lack of sensitivity or timing on the part of the counselor. In fact, if you are doing some very intense work with a client, he or she might become frightened of what is emerging and stop the process as a form of self-protection. Some of this makes sense because your client may have been psychologically and physically hurt in the past and resorted to defenses as a way to cope with an intolerable situation. Therefore this person may be overdefensive and guarded lest he or she be re-wounded. Exploring these fears is precisely what may be needed for a client to be able to break out of a restricted mode of existence. If you are reluctant to address resistance in your clients, they will also be hesitant to address ways they might be resisting the process. There will be times when you are not sure whether there are reality-based reasons for clients not showing up for appointments or if this is indicative of resistance. However, if you consistently approach what looks like resistance with respect and concern, you increase the chances your client will explore this behavior.

BECOMING THE CLIENT: Experiencing Resistance in Yourself

I want to invite you again to assume the role of client and imagine that you and I are engaged in a therapeutic relationship. I am presenting some key ideas about the experience of resistance in this way because I believe you will come to appreciate the inevitable place of resistance in the therapeutic process if you allow yourself to consider ways you might resist when you are anxious.

I strongly encourage you to involve yourself in personal counseling if you plan to become a professional counselor. You are apt to learn a great deal about interventions that are both helpful and unproductive through your experience as a client. If you and your therapist work well together, you will also learn quite a bit about how you present yourself to the world. You are bound to respect the courage it takes to forge ahead even though you are frightened, particularly at those times when you wonder if the gain is worth some of the pain you might be experiencing. In Chapter 10, when we consider the topics of transference and countertransference, I will go into greater detail on the importance of you opening yourself to some form of personal self-exploration—such as individual counseling, group counseling, family therapy, or some other pathway toward self-understanding. For now, let me encourage you to be as open as you can in imagining yourself in the role of a client in counseling with me as you deal with your own ways of resisting.

I will assign a variety of resistances to you in this section and show how I might intervene. Let yourself get into the role of actually experiencing the various forms of resistance. Some of these scenarios will not fit you, and you may have other inventive ways of resisting that I do not describe. See what you can learn about yourself by placing yourself in the center of resistance.

If you and I are involved in a client/therapist relationship, my main endeavor is to create and maintain the kind of working relationship that will allow you to take significant risks. Part of this relationship means that I must recognize the signs of resistance, both in you and in myself. If you and I are not dealing well with resistance, it may be a sign that our relationship needs strengthening. (Refer to Chapter 2 on the therapeutic relationship as the foundation for effective counseling for more on this topic.)

The ways you might resist are many, some subtle and others more obvious. Ask yourself if you might engage in any of these resistances:

- Forgetting about your counseling appointment
- Frequently showing up late for your sessions
- Not having material to bring into the sessions
- Complaining that you are not being helped by counseling
- Being silent and expecting to be drawn out
- Becoming defensive when your therapist gives you feedback
- Engaging in long-winded stories and leaving out how you are feeling
- Doing a great deal of intellectualizing about why you feel the way you do
- Avoiding emotional expression
- Striving very hard to please the therapist
- Talking in the abstract and remaining global
- Depending on the therapist excessively

Some of these behaviors may be anchored in reality and be a realistic and appropriate response. For instance, your defensiveness regarding feedback from your therapist may be a function of how the therapist presents the feedback to you. Everything that looks like resistance may not actually be resistance. This is why resistance needs to be explored and its meaning sensitively discussed. What are some other ways that you might resist?

Consider that you are coming for one of the early sessions of counseling with me. During this first counseling session, are you experiencing any reluctance? What will you talk about at the first session? I ask why you are coming in for counseling at this time. How do you reply? If you are like many in the helping professions, you might have trouble asking for help for yourself. Do you think you should be problem-free if you are going to be a good counselor? Do you have some pressing problems but feel that you should be able to resolve them on your own without any assistance from anyone?

How open are you? How much do you want from counseling? Students enrolled in counseling programs often go for counseling because it is required as part of the program or because they have been encouraged by their professors (or authors of their textbooks). Some of the resistances they often display can be summarized thusly: "Well, I'm not really sure I need therapy, but I suppose I could learn something about myself from coming in here. To be truthful, though, it is sort of difficult for me to ask for help. In many ways I think I should be able to deal with my problems by myself. After all, everyone has problems, so maybe I could get along fine without any counseling. Besides, I've got a lot going for me in my life, and things are great. If I go digging around, who knows what I might find out. Maybe it would be better not to open any can of worms and let good enough be!"

Now I don't expect you or any client to say this much as an opening statement, but it does illustrate some of the ambivalence I see in counseling students when they present themselves for personal counseling. Reflect for a moment about some of the ambivalence you might be experiencing if you came to counseling because of the urging of your professors or mainly to meet a requirement of your program.

It will be beneficial to spend some time exploring some of your beliefs about seeking counseling for yourself. Do you think initiating counseling means that you are not in control of your life? Are you admitting that there is something wrong with you by going for counseling? We can certainly talk about these beliefs and how such beliefs might hinder your openness in this counseling relationship—and how these beliefs might hinder you as a counselor. Talk about what you are experiencing as you come into this session today. Are you feeling excited? Anxious? Hopeful? Frightened? Cautious? Eager? I will continue to center my questions around your feelings, especially if you are experiencing hesitation, to get to the core reasons for your resistance.

Let's imagine we work well together and you decide there are some areas of your life in which you feel somewhat stuck and want to understand more fully. Assume this is the fifth session, and you bring up for discussion the gulf that you sense between you and your father. You tell me: "My Dad has never really been emotionally available to me, and I still miss this. You'd think that by this time I should have gotten over needing approval and affection from my father. The truth is there are times when I realize I'm still looking to others for what I've missed with my Dad. I still remember when I was a child and how much I wanted him to notice me and tell me I was special. But I felt he never really knew me and wasn't too interested in spending time with me." Now, if you had shared this with me, there would be plenty of rich material to pursue here. But let's assume that with every question I pose you draw a blank. You have little to say and seem emotionally reserved. There are long pauses, and many times you grow silent. You give only terse responses to my inquiries. Can you imagine any of this happening?

There are many reasons you might not be ready to work and why you may be hesitant. I want to know about these reasons, but I also want you to understand your own reluctance. Then you can decide whether you are willing to change some of your defensive patterns. Resistance typically occurs when a person begins to approach painful or threatening material that, if revealed, would result in feelings of vulnerability. It makes sense that you are not eager to experience feelings of shame, vulnerability, and uncertainty. At the same time, I want to be consistent in inviting you to address the ways you may be holding back. When you get close to painful experiences and become frightened, do you try to avoid these feelings by some kind of diversion? I will encourage you to challenge your tendency to flee and even go deeper into the feeling or behavior you wish to avoid. In my view, facing and experiencing feelings takes courage. Your willingness to endure the pain that is often necessary for getting unstuck and making way for new growth is a reflection of that courage.

Regarding the long pauses and your short answers, I would most certainly ask what is going on inside of you that you are not expressing. You appear to be censoring your thoughts and carefully editing what you verbally express. I might say any or all of these things: "I'd hope you will rehearse out loud." "You are quiet, yet it seems like a lot is going on in your head. Are you willing to put words to any of this?" "I'm noticing that you give short answers, that you think a long time before replying, and that you seem to be very cautious. What is it like to be in here now? How free do you feel to put to words what is on your mind and in your heart?"

I am not too quick to make the assumption that your silences are a sure sign of resistance. What makes it difficult for you to speak? Your silence could be related to any number of factors. Are you figuring out what you think I want to hear? Are you hesitant to speak because it will open the flood gates of emotion? Are you waiting for me to comment more on what you say before you speak? You might be trying very hard to figure out what is going on inside of you. I cannot know what keeps you quiet unless you eventually talk about it. Without labeling what you are doing as resistance, I point out what I see you doing and invite you to comment on what this means to you. I am trying to open a dialogue regarding what you are thinking and feeling as you sit in this session.

At this point I invite you to participate in a Gestalt experiment. I suggest that you bring what you are experiencing with your father into the room at this moment: "There is an empty chair over here. Would you be that child who so much wanted to be noticed and wanted Dad's approval and tell him that now? He is sitting in that chair and is ready to listen to what you have wanted to say." Your response is a flat refusal! Although I am not invested in forcing you to participate in any particular technique, I am interested in exploring with you why you won't see where this experiment leads. Talking about what is holding you back seems very crucial to me. You respond to my questioning in one of these ways:

- It really seems stupid talking to an empty chair. I would feel foolish doing that.
- I'm afraid of doing what you ask because just thinking about it brings tears to my eyes.
- I'd rather just tell you about my father because it would feel weird for me to talk to him when he is really not here.

Talking about what your reluctance means to you is one way to make this setting safer for you. If you'd feel foolish, I ask what would it would be like for you to feel foolish in my presence. This could tap useful material. If you indicate you don't want to put your father in the empty chair and talk to him because just imagining this brings you to tears, I follow that lead more fully. What are you crying about? How is it for you to get close to sadness at this moment? If I am able to understand the purpose your resistance serves and respect your hesitation, you will be more likely to come to a new understanding of your defensiveness. I want to show you that I am willing to go as far as you are and that I will not push you to do what you say you do not want to do. Ultimately, you decide which topics you are willing to pursue and how far you will go. By exploring your anxiety underlying an apparent resistance, the soil is being prepared for you to explore in more depth.

In another session let's assume that you begin with: "Today I want to talk about the tough time I am having in getting over being rejected in a relationship. Some days I think I'm fine, and other days I really get depressed and start thinking all sorts of horrible things about myself." Well, this is a rich lead, and there are many ways to work with it. Depending on the context of what you are describing, I might pursue a cognitive path with you, or encourage you to get more in contact with the feelings you are experiencing, or talk with you about actual courses of action you might take in doing something different. In fact, in one session it is very possible that we would work with what you are telling yourself about this breakup (cognitions and self-talk). I'd invite you to stay with feelings that are surfacing as you talk and suggest some behavioral steps you can take in moving in a different direction.

But what if you have mixed reactions about engaging in a dialogue on any level? What if your resistances are getting the best of you and you don't seem to be getting far in working cognitively, emotionally, or behaviorally? Put yourself in the following scenarios and imagine these ways you would resist.

You feel devastated over this breakup. This is proof of your unlovability. I suggest that you examine the validity of some of your conclusions. You reply that you should have gotten over this by now. As you reveal some of what you tell yourself about the breakup, I notice you tearing up, yet smiling at the same time. I describe what I'm noticing, and you withdraw. I suggest that you talk more about feeling rejected. Instead you provide an intellectual discussion about the tentative nature of interpersonal relationships and come up with a number of truisms such as "Life deals some difficult blows" and "Nothing ventured, nothing gained." I notice the ways I see you resisting, and I invite you to say more. For instance, what might happen if you were to allow yourself to feel the intensity of what you are feeling about the loss of this relationship—without smiling and without giving intellectual explanations? Following your resistance in a gentle but insistent manner could free you of the impasse you are experiencing. I am not at all sure where your exploration will lead if I ask you to stay with whatever avoidances emerge, yet I have a hunch that doing so will be productive. I encourage you to let down some unnecessary defenses but not to strip away all of your defenses. This process must be done respectfully and carefully, yet persistently.

There is more I'd like to do with you as a client pertaining to handling resistance, however there are limitations of doing this on the printed page. Let yourself reflect on some of the main ways you are likely to resist when your anxiety surfaces. Perhaps you can do some of this work by writing in your journal. Imagine all the ways you might resist when you are threatened psychologically. What are some defenses you rely on? What are examples of defenses you have used when you are feeling vulnerable? How did this work for you? Knowing what you do of yourself, to what extent do you think you would challenge your resistance? I hope you don't think courage means that you are without any fear. Courage means being afraid yet plunging ahead anyway. At points in your therapy you may become hesitant because you are afraid of your emerging feelings. How could you remain in the moment longer when your initial tendency is to withdraw? As you read about Ruth's case, see if you can identify with her resistance.

UNDERSTANDING RUTH'S RESISTANCE

See Session 5 (Understanding and Dealing With Resistance) of the *Student Video and Workbook for the Art of Integrative Counseling.*

As Ruth's therapy progresses, I expect some resistance—hesitation, defenses, and barriers—at certain anxiety-provoking points. Growth and change, even when positive, can involve discomfort. Ruth has conflicting aspects within her personality. Although a large part of Ruth would like to change, she fears the implications of changing. I want Ruth to know that resistance is not just something to be overcome, nor is it something for which I am judging her. Resistance is representative of familiar defensive approaches she uses in daily life. Ruth needs to recognize her resistance as a defensive strategy to cope with anxiety. It is also well for her to learn that her defenses interfere with her ability to accept change in a direction that could result in living a fuller and more gratifying life.

I want to do my best to respect Ruth's genuine concerns about moving forward. If handled properly, resistance can be one of the most valuable tools Ruth can use in her quest for self-understanding. Rather than fighting Ruth's initial resistance or hesitation, it is best to view it as a positive sign of strength. Ruth's defenses have worked for her to some degree, and at one time certain defenses may have enabled her to survive psychologically. Originally, Ruth's defenses served her in adapting to very difficult life circumstances. Her defenses were her best attempt to deal with conflicting situations at an earlier period of development. It is important for Ruth to realize that she is now capable of far more creative and healthier responses to the challenges she faces.

Overall, Ruth is a willing and motivated client. She is insightful, courageous, able to make connections between current behavior and past influences, willing to try risky behaviors both in the session and out of the session, and willing to face difficult issues in her life. Even under such favorable and almost ideal circumstances, it is not uncommon for her to experience some resistance and to entertain doubts about the value of counseling. To some extent it is healthy to resist in that it shows that she is aware of the risks of changing and the anxiety that is associated with coming to terms with unknown parts of herself. In one of her sessions, Ruth discusses whether to continue therapy. She exhibits some resistance in the form of not wanting to be in the therapy session. She is realizing that many in her family are not liking the changes she is making. Ruth recalls me telling her that she might get worse before she gets better. From her vantage point, this is exactly what is happening at home. Things are getting worse, which is causing her to doubt the value of what she is doing in counseling.

Borrowing From a Psychoanalytic View

In psychoanalytic practice resistance is anything that works against the progress of therapy and prevents the client from producing previously unconscious material. Ruth's resistance can be understood in the context of the intolerable anxiety and pain that she fears might arise if she were to become aware of feelings that are locked up inside of her. Her defenses are a way to protect herself from this anxiety as she faces truths about herself.

Because her resistance blocks threatening material from entering awareness, I ask her to talk about what her resistance means to her. I am first interested in her interpretation about how she is dealing with threatening situations, and perhaps later I will offer my hunches. I may point out what appears to be operating with a set of defenses to Ruth. I will also support her in facing her fears. At times I will suggest an interpretation in the form of a hunch so Ruth can become aware of the reasons for her resistances, which will allow her to deal with them. For example, "Let me share a hunch about what I see going on and see what you think of it. What we've been talking about is really scary for you. Meeting with all this flack and getting your family riled up over your changes is certainly not comfortable for you. This has temporarily gotten the best of you, and you seem to want to give up." Ruth can then reflect on the feedback I offer her and decide how accurate and useful my impressions of her are. By sharing a hunch with Ruth about the possible meanings a certain behavior may hold, I hope to deal with signs of resistance in a collaborative, nonjudgmental, nonthreatening, and respectful manner.

Drawing on Other Approaches

My goal is not to eliminate Ruth's resistance but to invite her to explore it. Most clients will be ambivalent, defensive, and hesitant at some point in the counseling process. This push-pull is occurring with Ruth and could result in premature termination of therapy if she does not discuss her fears and reservations about being in counseling. Although Ruth is externalizing her concerns by focusing on her husband's displeasure over her changes and the negative reactions from her children, internal factors may also be affecting Ruth and contributing to her resistance. Ruth is really split. Part of her wants to cling to the status quo, whereas another part of her wants to branch out and become more of the person she would like to be. I ask her to voice her doubts about the value of therapy. It is clear that she is ambivalent. Talking about Ruth's reluctance to participate fully in therapy can be done in a gentle yet confrontational way, along with providing support to face issues that she might otherwise avoid.

Later in the session I suggest we work with her ambivalence over wanting to change and resisting change. Using a Gestalt technique, I suggest a role play. I ask Ruth to play the side of her that wants to remain the same because that is the feeling that seems to be the strongest in her now. I take on the role of the side of Ruth that wants to move forward. In this role play we debate the pros and cons of changing. I do my best to highlight the advantages of taking the risks involved in making significant life changes. Ruth has an opportunity to express out loud what she tends to rehearse silently about the guarantees of sticking with the "old version" of Ruth. After engaging in this role play for a time, I ask Ruth what she is experiencing. We then reverse roles so that she can deepen her experience of the splits within her. After switching roles for a time, Ruth decides that a larger part of her wants to stay in therapy, even though it seems to be causing chaos at home.

Toward the end of the session Ruth admits that she had not realized how scared she has become, yet she adds that preserving the status quo isn't working for her either. It has become clear to her that she is caught in a rut and experiences life as being stale. She really wants more from her life, yet she is frightened when she considers what she might have to do or become to have a more satisfying existence. Because I accept the existential notion of the client's place in choosing how far to go, it is Ruth who makes the choices pertaining to facing her reluctance to make some basic changes in her life.

The feminist therapy approach reminds me of how crucial it is for Ruth to be an active participant in her counseling and to make her own choices. I am committed to ensuring that our therapeutic relationship does not become another arena in which Ruth stays in a passive, dependent role. It is important that Ruth give voice to her experiencing now. Initially, she tended to look to me for answers or advice. As I continued to place the responsibility back on her, and to relate to her more as a person than as an "expert," she experienced glimpses of what it is like to trust more in her own power. She is beginning to get in touch with a range of feelings, including anger and other "prohibited" emotions she learned to deny to herself. Some of Ruth's self-doubts and anxiety over continuing in therapy relate to a host of feelings that she has kept in check but that are now emerging within her. I want Ruth to feel that it is acceptable to talk openly about her anxiety over experiencing these "new" feelings.

At this point I attempt to pull together some of the conflicting themes we've talked about in the session and invite Ruth to reflect on where she wants to go from here. I suggest a homework assignment, as I frequently do, with the expectation that Ruth will gain greater clarity of the options open to her and the choices she is willing to make. (Here I draw on behavior therapy, reality therapy, and rational emotive behavior therapy.) For one week I ask Ruth to write in her journal all the reasons for staying the same versus the reasons for making changes. I ask Ruth to reflect, for one day, on what her life might be like if she quits therapy and to think about the kind of life she might have if she continues on the path she has pursued for much of her life. On another day I ask Ruth to write in her journal about how she imagines her life could be if she continues with her therapy and makes some of the changes she desires. Ruth agrees to follow through with this homework, which gives us a good place to continue in a subsequent session.

GUIDELINES FOR DEALING WITH RESISTANCE IN CLIENTS

By putting yourself in the role of the client I hope you have come to appreciate how challenging the counseling process can be. I suspect that some of your most valuable lessons on how to recognize, understand, and deal with resistance in your clients will be learned from your own experience with personal counseling. In addition to encouraging you to formulate your own perspective on the role of resistance in the counseling process, here are a few suggestions for you to consider when you meet with any hesitation on a client's part.

- Think of resistance as a normal process involving a lack of readiness on a client's part to get involved in counseling. Work with the resistance rather than fight it.

- If you label certain behaviors your clients display as "resistance," they might feel judged and begin to think of resistance as something totally negative. A useful way to view resistance, and to assist clients in recognizing its manifestations, is by thinking it as the lack of readiness to engage in therapeutic work.
- Realize that initially many clients are defensive about having to meet with you to deal with their problems. Simply coming in for counseling may be a sign of weakness in their minds, which may make them hesitant to be open.
- It is important to understand the many meanings of client resistance and not to interpret it as evidence of your professional incompetence. If you are focused on defending yourself against the various forms of resistance you encounter with clients, you deprive them of opportunities to explore the meanings of their resistance.
- Encourage clients to explore any form of resistance rather than demanding that they give up their resistance.
- State your observations, hunches, and interpretations in a tentative way rather than making dogmatic pronouncements.
- Avoid labeling and judging a client, and instead describe the behavior the individual is displaying. Let your client know how he or she is affecting you in a nonblaming and noncritical way.
- Distinguish between the phenomenon of resistance, which is occurring in your client, and your reactions to the client's resistance. Monitor your reactions so that you don't escalate client resistance.
- Deal with resistance in a positive way. If you accept your client and do not react defensively, this will probably melt the intensity of the client's resistance. If you meet resistance with resistance, you are likely to entrench this pattern.
- Allow clients to express their feelings about prior negative experiences with counseling. Ask them what they would like to do differently with you.
- Provide clients with a brief explanation of how you work and strive to obtain genuine informed consent. Educate clients about ways they can use the relationship with you to help themselves.
- Let clients know that counseling often entails some setbacks. If they know from the beginning that personal learning is not always a smooth path, they are less likely to react with discouragement when they experience a plateau or a relapse.
- Strive to arrive together at a clear statement of the problem or the reason the client seeks counseling at this particular time. As soon as possible, design interventions in small, manageable steps that lead to a satisfactory solution.

CONCLUDING COMMENTS

Resistance is not an enemy to be feared or a therapeutic evil to be eliminated; it is the very substance of the therapeutic process. To better understand the role resistance plays and how best to deal with it, be open to identifying resistive patterns within yourself. Remember your difficulty in being open to your own growth, and use this as a model for understanding your clients. If you keep in mind how you deal with resistance, you will be less likely to personalize client resistance.

As a way to identify how you deal with resistance in yourself, take some time at this point to reflect on the following questions:

- When you consider yourself in the role of a counseling client, what might lead to resistance for you? What are some of the ways in which you are most likely to resist? What kind of resistive behaviors might you use?
- When you have experienced resistance, can you remember some of your bodily reactions? What kind of self-talk goes on within you when you experience resistance?
- What might help you to reduce your level of resistance or defensiveness? What would you want from your counselor when you are resistant?
- Having finished this chapter, take a few minutes to consolidate your thinking about resistance. What is your definition of resistance? As a counselor, what will help you to understand and deal with any resistance you might encounter from clients?
- Imagine a resistant and difficult client sitting in your office. Let yourself imagine the characteristics of this client. How does this client affect you? What kind of resistive behavior do you think you would be most challenged by as a counselor? What kind of client is most likely to bring out your defensive reactions? Can you learn anything about yourself by paying attention to your reactions to your most difficult client?

6

Cognitive Focus in Counseling

All integrative approaches make room for the cognitive dimension—we are all thinking beings. I pay a great deal of attention to thinking as a vital component in counseling because the content of thought processes greatly influences both how we feel and how we act. An integrative approach requires dealing with self-talk, faulty thinking, core beliefs, and one's worldview. I find many aspects of the cognitive behavioral therapies (CBT) very valuable in my work, both during therapy sessions and in a variety of everyday life situations. Therapy is essentially a teaching and learning process, which makes cognitive and behavioral methods most relevant.

Cognitive behavioral approaches are very diverse. Two main forms include rational emotive behavior therapy (REBT), developed by Albert Ellis (1999), and cognitive therapy (CT), developed by Aaron Beck (see Alford & Beck, 1997; J. Beck, 1995). Both of these approaches place thinking at the core of emotional and behavioral disturbances. Their differences lie mainly in the style a therapist employs. Both CT and REBT are based on the assumption that if we change our thinking we can also change our feelings and the way we act. In these approaches the client must be active if change is to occur. Clients work collaboratively with the therapist, assuming the role of a learner in the therapy sessions and being willing to involve themselves in homework they practice in daily life.

The Benefits and Limitations of a Cognitive Focus

If you were seeking therapy with me, I would be interested in what you think, believe, and the way in which you perceive the world. Your basic beliefs may be the product of considerable reflection and questioning, or you may have acquired a number of beliefs without critically evaluating them. In either case, how you feel and what you do in certain situations has a lot to do with your basic beliefs and thought patterns. Some beliefs may serve you well, whereas others may lead to problems for you.

Significant others in your past contributed to shaping your current lifestyle, but you are responsible for maintaining self-destructive ideas and attitudes that influence your daily transactions. As your therapist, I see value in confronting you with questions such as: "What are your assumptions and basic beliefs? Have you really examined the core ideas you live by to determine if they are your own values or merely introjects, that is, beliefs you have uncritically acquired from others?" Adlerian therapy, rational emotive behavior therapy, cognitive therapy, and choice theory/reality therapy share the basic assumption that situational events do not have the power to determine you. Rather, it is your interpretation of these events that is crucial. Instead of talking about events, therapists with a cognitive focus explore the personal meanings you attach to these events.

Although clients benefit from a cognitive understanding of their problems, an overemphasis on the cognitive realm can shortchange the emotive dimension. For instance, it may be difficult for you to get in contact with your feelings or even to identify what you are feeling. Because of the anxiety of staying with painful emotions, you might use some form of deflection and engage in intellectualizing. If you too quickly try to figure out why you are feeling a certain way, you may avoid facing whatever you are feeling. For example, if you don't get a job that you want, you might engage in self-deception and rationalizations over why you didn't really want the job in the first place rather than experiencing your feelings and appropriately expressing them in the here and now.

Approaches that highlight cognition typically do not give much attention to exploring a client's past emotional issues. If you and I are working within a cognitive framework, I would pay attention to your past without getting lost in the past and without assuming a fatalistic stance about earlier traumatic experiences. Past unresolved childhood experiences can be fruitfully explored in therapy if these earlier experiences are connected to your present level of functioning. Painful early experiences need to be recognized, felt fully, reexperienced, and worked through in therapy before you can free yourself of their restrictive influences. Present beliefs about yourself and your current problems are often related to past wounding. Unless you come to terms with these past traumas, the vestiges of these traumas tend to linger in the background and influence your current ways of being.

I question the view of most cognitive behavioral therapies that exploring the past is not useful or effective in helping clients change faulty thinking and behavior. I think the cognitive behavioral approaches work best once you have identified and dealt with your emotional issues. In practice, I don't see how it is really possible to work exclusively in a cognitive way, or an emotive way, or a behavioral way. As you will see in Ruth's case, by dealing with certain core beliefs she becomes emotionally touched and experiences various bodily sensations. In other words, when Ruth thinks, she also feels and acts. When she acts, she feels and thinks. When she feels, she thinks and acts. Cognition, emotion, and behavior are not separate human functions. They are interactive and integrated. (The theory that offers the most insight here is reality therapy with its concept of total behavior. According to reality therapy, every behavior includes all three components.)

BECOMING THE CLIENT: Experiencing Cognitive Behavioral Techniques

To be most creatively applied, cognitive and behavioral strategies must be tailored to the client's unique needs and situation. To increase cooperation, it is important to respect client reactions to an intervention. These interventions are tools to be used in service of the client. Here are a few cognitive behavioral techniques from my integrative approach that I might employ with you as my client.

Paying Attention to Your Thinking

Do you engage in catastrophic thinking? Do you dwell on the most extreme negative scenarios in many situations? When you get stuck, imagine the worst possible outcome of the situation. Then ask, "What is the worst thing that could occur? If this happens, what would make this such a negative outcome?" You can learn to engage in more realistic thinking, especially if you consistently notice times when you tend to get caught up in catastrophic thinking.

Assisting you to look for evidence to support or refute some of your core beliefs can be most useful. Once you identify a number of self-defeating beliefs, you can begin to monitor the frequency with which these beliefs intrude in situations in everyday life. This simple question can be frequently asked of you during counseling sessions: "Where is the evidence for___?" Make it a practice to ask yourself this question, especially as you become more adept at spotting dysfunctional thoughts and paying attention to your cognitive patterns. For example, the statement "I *must* be approved of and accepted by all the significant people in my life" can be disputed with statements such as "Where is it written that I *must* have this approval?" "Why *must* I have their total approval to feel like a worthwhile individual?" An effective and functional belief might include this statement: "There is no evidence that I *absolutely must* have approval from others, though I would like to be approved of by those whom I respect." You might also tell yourself, "I really cannot stand rejection, so I must keep to myself so I won't be hurt." How would this belief affect the way you respond to others? I would ask you: "Even though rejection would hurt, would it be catastrophic? How might this fear of being rejected keep you from getting what you want in your relationships?" At this point make a list of statements that might get in your way at times. What are a few examples of basic conclusions that you could challenge?

Doing Homework Assignments

The cognitive behavioral approaches place considerable emphasis on putting newly acquired insights into action. Homework assignments enable you to practice new behaviors and assist you in the process of your reconditioning. The therapy hour is limited, and activities designed to be continued outside the office can augment therapy sessions. The best homework consists of activities suggested by the client, especially self-help assignments that grow out of the previous session. It is essential that homework assignments be tailored to your specific problems and that these activities be collaboratively developed by both of us. Again, let me stress that homework or any intervention is geared to what you want for yourself, not what I, as your therapist, think you should want—or what I want for you.

After you have identified some unsupported conclusions and faulty beliefs, between therapy sessions record and think about how your beliefs contribute to your personal problems. In this way you can work hard at critically examining your self-defeating cognitions. When you come to the next therapy session, bring up specific situations in which you did well or in which you experienced difficulty. As you consistently question the actual evidence for situations you encounter, you become more effective in challenging your self-talk. This allows you to determine whether your self-statements are based on accurate or erroneous information.

I will teach you ways to carry on your own therapy, largely through homework activities, without my direct intervention. This provides you with tools you can use to continue learning once formal counseling ends. In my view, much of our counseling endeavor will deal with educating you, teaching you coping skills, and enabling you to see the connection between what you are learning in the therapy office and everyday living. I particularly value the emphasis CBT puts on bibliotherapy and psychoeducational assignments such as listening to tapes, reading self-help books, keeping a record of what you are doing and thinking, and attending workshops. In this way you can further the process of change in yourself without becoming excessively dependent on me as your counselor. It will be useful to review psychoeducational assignments with you to assess the value of such assignments.

Drawing on Adlerian Concepts

Adlerian psychology pays particular attention to the cognitive aspects of personality and in many ways can be considered a cognitive approach to counseling. For Adlerians feelings are aligned with thinking and are the fuel for behaving. Working within an Adlerian framework, my assumption is that first you think, then you feel, and then you act. Because emotions and cognitions serve a purpose and aim at a central goal in your life, much of our time during counseling will be spent discovering and understanding your purpose and reorienting you in a useful way. You can expect to explore what Adlerians call "private logic," which includes concepts about yourself, others, and your life. The core of the therapy experience consists of discovering the purposes of your behavior or symptoms and the basic mistakes associated with your coping.

In therapy let's assume we discover that the structure of your private logic is captured by this syllogism:

- I am basically unlovable.
- The world is filled with people who are likely to reject unlovable persons.
- Therefore, I must keep to myself so I won't be discovered and rejected.

With further exploration you and I find these central themes or convictions in your life:

- I must get what I want in life.
- I must control everything in my life.
- I must know everything there is to know, and a mistake would be catastrophic.
- I must be perfect in everything I do.

It is easy to see how depression or a sense of hopelessness might follow from this thinking. Learning how to correct such faulty assumptions and conclusions will be central to your therapy. Through the therapeutic process, you will discover that you have resources and options to draw on in dealing with significant life issues and life tasks.

The Adlerian approach offers me a great deal of freedom in working with a range of problems. I can use my clinical judgment in applying a wide range of techniques that appear to work best for you in your particular situation. The Adlerian concepts I draw from most as part of my integrative model are (1) the importance of looking to one's life goals, including assessing how these goals influence an individual; (2) the focus on the individual's interpretation of early experiences in the family, with special emphasis on their current impact; (3) the clinical use of early recollections; (4) the need to understand and confront basic mistakes; (5) the cognitive emphasis, which holds that emotions and behaviors are largely influenced by one's beliefs and thinking processes; (6) the idea of working out an action plan designed to help clients make changes; (7) the collaborative relationship, whereby client and therapist work toward mutually agreed-on goals; and (8) the emphasis given to encouragement during the entire counseling process (Nystul, 1999a). These Adlerian concepts all have implications for personal development.*

WORKING WITH RUTH FROM A COGNITIVE PERSPECTIVE

See Session 6 (Cognitive Focus in Counseling) of the *Student Video and Workbook for the Art of Integrative Counseling.*

My integrative approach in counseling Ruth involves exploring her *cognitive structures,* which include her belief systems, her thoughts, her

---

* For further reading on integrating cognitive therapy in your counseling orientation, I suggest you consult Alford and Beck (1997), Beck (1995), Ellis (1999), and Ellis and MacLaren (1998). For a general treatment of cognitive perspectives, see Corey, 2001c, Chapters 5 and 11.

attitudes, and her values. More specifically, in family systems therapy attention is given to family rules; in behavior therapy attention is given to beliefs and assumptions that have an influence on her behavior. In rational emotive behavior therapy attention is on self-defeating beliefs and self-indoctrination; Adlerian therapy focuses on her basic mistakes and faulty thinking. In reality therapy the emphasis may be on Ruth's values and what she wants in her world; in feminist therapy I would conduct an assessment of the impact of gender-role messages (which is discussed in more detail in Chapter 12). Whatever terms are used, I tend to zero in on the underlying messages that Ruth seems to be hearing now in her life. I assume that her self-talk is relevant to her behavior.

From a cognitive behavioral perspective I examine the ways in which Ruth's internal dialogue and her thinking processes are affecting her day-to-day behavior. I will use an active and directive therapeutic style. Therapy will be time-limited, present-centered, solution-focused, and structured. My task is to help Ruth recognize and change her self-defeating thoughts and maladaptive beliefs. We will concentrate on the content and process of her thinking by looking for ways to restructure some of her beliefs.

Rather than merely telling Ruth what faulty beliefs she has, I will encourage her to gather data and weigh the evidence in support of certain beliefs. Through a Socratic dialogue, Ruth and I will be able to identify where her thinking, feeling, and behaving is problematic. I will assist her in detecting her faulty thinking, in learning ways of correcting her distortions, and in substituting more effective self-talk and beliefs. Here are a few of the questions I raise for Ruth to ponder and to answer: "What do you suppose it would be like if you were not to live up to the standards others have set for you?" "If you remain the way you are now, what do you imagine your life will be like in a few years?" "How might you feel different if you were able to ease up on yourself?" We will be using a wide range of cognitive, emotive, and behavioral techniques to accomplish our goals.

A main cognitive technique I will use with Ruth is disputing faulty beliefs. Much of Ruth's therapy involves her learning ways to argue with her internal dialogue. Here are some questions aimed at getting Ruth to examine the evidence for the validity of her beliefs: "Does having this belief help or hinder you in your life?" "Where is the evidence for your belief?" "Who told you that this belief is accurate?" Not only will I introduce debating methods during the therapy hour, but I'll encourage Ruth to pay attention to her internal dialogue in daily life and to detect patterns of thinking that become problematic for her. She can then argue with her internal voices when she catches herself getting stuck or reverting to old patterns. I am especially inclined to employ cognitive interventions when it appears that Ruth is giving in to internal voices that reinforce a stance of powerlessness. Such techniques are called for in situations where Ruth might make dire predictions about her future, when such conclusions are based on negative beliefs.

My interventions are aimed at getting Ruth to reflect on what she is saying and how this is influencing how she is feeling. My hope is that Ruth will explore the facts involved in these situations, that she will take another look at some of the conclusions she has arrived at, and that she will develop an open stance in assessing new situations. My aim is to get Ruth to think about her thinking and how it has a pervasive influence on her life today. In dealing with Ruth's cognitions from an Adlerian perspective, I might focus Ruth's attention on messages she incorporated as a child and on the decisions that she made. Eventually, I get her to think about the reasons she made certain early decisions. I challenge her to look at these decisions about life, about herself, and about others and to make necessary revisions that can lead her to form new assumptions about life. The topic of early decisions and redecisions is elaborated on in Chapter 12.

From rational emotive behavior therapy (REBT) I especially value the emphasis on learning to think rationally. I look for ways Ruth contributes to her negative feelings by the process of self-indoctrination with faulty beliefs. I get her to really test the validity of the dire consequences she predicts. For example, Ruth is extremely self-critical, she demands perfection, she believes that she *must* live up to what others expect of her at all times, and she drives herself by performance-oriented standards to the point of exhaustion. I value the stress put on doing hard work in uprooting beliefs that have no validity and replacing them with sound and realistic beliefs. Ruth must find for herself a new set of beliefs that allow her to enjoy life more fully. It is not my place to provide her with realistic and appropriate beliefs, but I work with her in creating constructive beliefs of her own. I do not think she can think her way through life or that examining her faulty logic is enough by itself for personality change, but I do see this process as an essential component of therapy.

Ruth believes that everything she does has to be perfect. In essence, she has convinced herself that she must be the perfect daughter, the perfect wife, the perfect mother, and the perfect student. Ruth has an underlying dysfunctional belief that she must be perfect in all that she attempts. If she is not perfect, in her mind, there are dire results. She is continually rating her performances, and she is bound to think poorly of herself because of her unrealistically high standards. Indeed, there is a judge sitting on her shoulder. I will consistently remind Ruth that rating herself as a person will take her on a path toward misery. Although Ruth might continue to rate some of her actions, she can productively reflect on separating what she is doing from her personhood. Global and harsh self-ratings are not helpful to her in the long run and only serve to reinforce her self-condemnation. I hope to teach Ruth practical ways to talk back to her internal critic, to learn a new and functional self-dialogue, and to help her reevaluate her experiences as she changes her behavior.

Ruth hears this underlying message, which was given to her by her mother: "If you can't do a job well, don't do it at all." Because she does not attain perfection, she frequently experiences frustration and guilt. As I am talking with Ruth about her perfectionism, she indicates that she wishes she could be kinder to herself and not feel and believe that she has to be perfect in every aspect of life. She says, "I'd like to ease up on myself."

I suggest a role play in which she plays the part of herself that would like to ease up and I play the part of her that is the critical and driving self. Whenever she indicates that she wants to do less and not push herself so hard, I tell her that she cannot afford to get lax.

One of the desired outcomes of counseling is for Ruth to become less self-critical. She has indicated that she would like to be easier on herself. My rationale for this cognitive role play with Ruth is to facilitate an examination on her part of what she believes and where she got her beliefs. My hope is that she will begin to question messages that she has uncritically accepted, then she can determine whether her beliefs are serving her at this point in her life. Through a process of debating, disputing, and critically examining some of the messages that Ruth lives by, Ruth will gain increased clarity of the many ways she is trying to measure up to external expectations. By arguing with me as I role-play a familiar side of her, she will be increasingly able to experience the depth to which her self-talk actually exhausts her. By staying with the dialogue for a time, Ruth becomes aware of how tired she is of always pushing herself. She says: "I am so tired of always having to measure up. I am just exhausted. But I don't know how to stop. I'm caught in a whirlwind and just don't know how to stop." Ruth admits that she feels very tired of striving to live up to expectations. What is interesting therapeutically is that Ruth gets a clearer picture of what she is doing and how it is affecting her. Although she does not want to pursue the path she is going down, she is at a loss to know how to stop or even slow down. Ruth becomes quite emotional as she talks about not knowing how to stop. She shares her exhaustion over always feeling that she has to measure up—and she adds that she just does not want to live this way anymore. Ruth is giving a clear message of wanting to make a basic change. Now we can use a host of interventions to help her change some of her core beliefs that lead to her exhaustion.

From the cognitive behavioral models, I accept the assumption that it is not an event or a situation in life that actually causes problematic emotions. Rather, it is the evaluation of events and the beliefs people hold about these events that get them into trouble. I listen attentively to Ruth's underlying assumptions as she participates in a role play with me to see if she has uncritically incorporated messages that are contributing to her high level of personal stress. I want Ruth to understand that when she is less than perfect in situations it is her perception and evaluation that contributes to her problems. Drawing from REBT, I have most likely explained to Ruth the ABC model, as developed by Albert Ellis (1999). In short, this concept holds that events do not directly result in a given set of consequences. I will teach Ruth the A-B-C theory of personality. This concept is based on the premise that **A** (the activating event) does not cause **C** (the emotional consequences); rather, it is mainly **B** (her belief about the activating event) that is the source of her problems. Much of my teaching will be about how Ruth can change **B** (her belief systems) and thereby make some significant emotional and behavioral changes.

My expectation is that Ruth will realize that her feelings of anxiety are not caused by particular events she is experiencing at home and in her program at the university. More than the activating events in her life, I do some teaching on the all-important role of Ruth's core beliefs as a contributing factor to undesirable emotional and behavioral outcomes. For instance, if all Ruth's children do very little for her but expect her to be "on call" whenever they want her, this very reality is not the factor that is causing Ruth's present psychological difficulties. The source of her problem is what she tells herself about the kind of inadequate mother she is. Ruth operates from the basic belief that if her "mothering skills" are less than perfect she is deficient as a person. In essence, she is making the mistake of globally rating herself as a person on the basis of some of her behaviors. My interventions are aimed at getting her to better understand the connection between some of her core beliefs and her ways of feeling and acting. I hope she can think about some of her basic assumptions and discover how her self-talk is influencing how she is feeling and what she is doing.

At some point in Ruth's therapy, it is likely that we will examine the validity of many of her interpretations about life situations and her conclusions about her basic worth. Beck's cognitive therapy emphasizes identifying and changing negative thoughts and maladaptive beliefs (also known as schemata). According to Beck's cognitive model of emotional disorders, to understand the nature of emotional problems it is essential to focus on the cognitive content of a client's reaction to an upsetting event or stream of thoughts (see J. Beck, 1995). I draw on a range of cognitive, emotive, and behavioral techniques to demonstrate to Ruth that she causes her own emotional disturbances by the faulty beliefs she has acquired. In this and other sessions, we explore what cognitive therapists call "cognitive distortions" (see Dattilio & Freeman, 1992), some of which are:

- *Arbitrary inferences.* Ruth makes conclusions without supporting and relevant evidence. She often engages in "catastrophizing," or thinking about the worst possible scenario for a given situation.
- *Overgeneralization.* Ruth holds extreme beliefs based on a single incident and applies them inappropriately to other dissimilar events or settings. For instance, because she and her husband are experiencing marital difficulties, she is convinced that she is a failure in all aspects of her marriage.
- *Personalization.* Ruth has a tendency to relate external events to herself, even when there is no basis for making this connection. She relates an incident in which a professor did not call on her in class, even though her hand was raised. She was convinced that her professor did not value her thoughts and was bothered by her. She did not consider any other possible explanations for the fact that she was not asked to state her ideas in this class meeting.
- *Labeling and mislabeling.* Ruth presents herself in light of her imperfections and mistakes. She allows a singular problem situation to define her total being.
- *Polarized thinking.* Ruth frequently engages in thinking and interpreting in all-or-nothing terms. Either she is a success as a mother or she is

> a total failure in mothering. Through this process of dichotomous thinking, she has created self-defeating labels and boxes that keep her restricted.

Over a number of sessions we work on specific beliefs. The aim is for Ruth to critically evaluate the evidence for many of her conclusions.

I view my role as promoting corrective experiences that will lead to changes in her thinking. I expect to assist her in discovering for herself how to distinguish between functional and dysfunctional beliefs. She can learn this by testing her conclusions. My assumption is that only through learning to apply rigorous self-challenging methods will she succeed in freeing herself from the self-defeating thinking that contributed to her problems. Although the cognitive dimension is emphasized, this cannot be accomplished without bringing in the behavioral dimension. Together we will design behavioral homework assignments that put Ruth in situations where she is challenged to confront her self-defeating beliefs and her self-limiting behavior. I also consistently challenge her to question her basic assumption that she needs the approval of others to feel adequate.*

CONCLUDING COMMENTS

Now that you have read this chapter, go back over some of the key themes I've identified from the cognitive approaches and apply them to yourself. Try to identify some of your basic convictions, core beliefs, and self-talk. Ask yourself where you acquired your basic beliefs and how they appear to be influencing the ways you feel and act today. What are some of the key concepts and techniques from the cognitive behavioral approaches that you most value in understanding yourself and in aiding you to restructure some of your problematic beliefs? How do you imagine it would be for you to be a client in cognitive behavioral therapy? After reflecting on the personal applications, ask yourself what you'd want to incorporate from this approach as a counselor. What concepts and techniques most fit into your personal philosophy of counseling?

---

* For a more detailed description of working with Ruth from a cognitive behavioral perspective, see my counseling with Ruth from this perspective and Albert Ellis's counseling with Ruth using REBT in Chapter 9 of *Case Approach to Counseling and Psychotherapy* (Corey, 2001b).

7

Emotive Focus in Counseling

In their useful book, *Facilitating Emotional Change: The Moment-by-Moment Process,* Greenberg, Rice, and Elliot (1993) present the theory and methods of an emotionally focused approach to counseling, which is oriented toward the construction of new emotional meaning. I recommend their book to get a sense of the experiential approach. The basis of this process-oriented experiential approach is the recognition that therapists need to be fully attentive to clients' present experience and expression. According to Greenberg and her colleagues, it is important for therapists to strive to see, hear, and understand clients' moment-by-moment experiencing. It is more important to facilitate this experiential process in clients than to strive to modify their cognitions or behaviors. When the therapist is able to affirm clients' experience, clients feel safe enough to generate new emotional meanings. In other words, the provision of an empathically attuned and respectful relationship provides the support necessary for clients to allow themselves to experience a range of feelings that they might otherwise block, which then allows them to modify their patterns of thinking and acting.

THE BENEFITS AND LIMITATIONS OF AN EMOTIVE FOCUS

Just as cognition is essential to an integrative counseling style, so is the emotional dimension. Too often—especially with brief therapy aimed at discovering solutions to problems as efficiently and quickly as possible—what clients are feeling is relegated to a secondary position. Even in brief therapy I would want to be open to exploring emotions. It can be a mistake to zero in on the cognitive realm and challenge mistaken beliefs before clients feel understood. Clients need to have an opportunity to talk before the therapist confronts their mode of thinking. Often the best route to getting clients to examine their cognitions is by encouraging them to identify, express, and deal with what they are feeling.

It can be tempting, however, to view the release of emotions as an end in itself. I value the role of catharsis in counseling, but I don't view this as the final aim of counseling. Following an emotional release, it is essential to work with the associated insights and the cognitions underlying the emotional patterns. It is important to link emotional exploration to cognitive and behavioral work.

Significant personal changes will come about only if clients are taught how to transfer what they have learned in therapy sessions to everyday situations. Transferring this learning is not an automatic process. Therapists must teach clients how to maintain these positive emotional and behavioral changes. This can be done by helping clients plan ways of coping effectively when they meet with frustration in the world and when they regress by seeming to forget the lessons they have learned. If therapy is aimed primarily at emotional release, without any kind of cognitive or behavioral follow up, clients will not acquire a method for transferring their learning to a range of situations in daily life.

BECOMING THE CLIENT: Experiencing Emotionally Focused Therapy

Generally, my preference is to begin therapy by paying attention to what you are experiencing on an emotional level, for this is where the energy is located. I pay attention to how emotions are manifested in your body. I think the truth of many of your struggles can be found in what you are feeling and what your body is telling you. I ask, "What are you aware of at the moment and what do you want to do with that?" Noticing your emotional and bodily states can be significant routes to gaining awareness of what you are experiencing and doing. Without awareness, change is impossible.

Gestalt therapy is a lively approach that promotes direct experiencing rather than the abstractness of talking about situations. You come to grips with *what* and *how* you are thinking, feeling, and acting as you interact with me as your therapist. I create and use techniques, or experiments, to facilitate the exploration of material that emerges from our interactions in the session. It is important that I pick up clues you give and design techniques that will help you understand how you are thinking, feeling, and behaving. I tend to avoid using planned techniques or exercises as catalysts to open up feelings. Experiments are more powerful when they grow out of the phenomenological context of therapy and when they are designed for a specific therapy situation as well as for my own personality and therapeutic style.

The techniques I select are geared to your thoughts, feelings, and actions and are tools to support your self-exploration. These tools have the purpose of facilitating your self-understanding, not promoting my personal agenda as your therapist or to meet my needs. It is extremely important that I use techniques with respect and concern for you as my client.

Gestalt experiments are designed to expand your awareness and to help you try out new modes of behavior. Experiments enable you to become aware of aspects of experience that had previously been out of awareness. Within the safety of the therapeutic situation, you are given opportunities to "try on" a new behavior. The Gestalt way of creating experiments is a powerful and effective way to connect you to your emotions. Although Gestalt therapy offers rich pathways to your emotional experiencing, this approach taps whatever is in your awareness at the moment and, in that sense, it is truly integrative.

As a way to demonstrate an experiential, emotionally focused approach, let me present you with some "issues" that I encourage you to "adopt" as my client. You tell me that what is in your awareness at this moment is that you feel a sense of sadness. I ask you to say more and to describe how you experience this sadness. You report the following: "I'm just feeling sad when I think of how hard I try to get approval from everyone. I'm so caught up in getting you to like me that I forget what it is I want for myself. I feel right now like I felt so much around my parents—always trying to do what they wanted so they would think well of me, yet never feeling that I was able to get what I wanted." You are saying a great deal, and I encourage you to keep talking. As you speak, I direct your attention to what you are experiencing in your body. You state that your heart is heavy and that it feels broken. I suggest that you stay with this bodily feeling as much as possible and put some words to what it is like for you to talk at this time. I might even ask you to give your heart a voice and give expression to your "heavy and broken heart." Where we go next depends on what emerges in your moment-to-moment awareness. I follow the leads you provide and support you in your efforts to stay focused on the images, feelings, thoughts, and sensations that come to the surface. I encourage you to stay with what *is* as fully as possible.

Operating within this experiential framework, I ask you to bring any concerns about what was or will be into the present and directly experience these concerns. Being in the present moment involves a transition between your past and your future. As a way to keep our work emotionally focused, I make use of Gestalt experiments that are spontaneously created to fit your present situation. Meaningful dialogue often results from staying with the changing flow of your present-centered awareness. By following whatever it is that you are experiencing and showing you how to follow your own energy, you will gradually expand your boundaries of awareness.

To help you make contact with the present moment, I typically ask "what" and "how" questions but rarely ask "why" questions. To promote "now" awareness, I encourage a dialogue in the present tense by asking "What is happening now? What is going on now? What are you experiencing as you share your struggle? What is your awareness at this moment? How are you experiencing your sadness? As you talk of your heavy heart, what is this like for you? If your heart could express itself, what would that be like for you?"

Now imagine yourself in this scenario. You say that you sometimes feel totally inadequate and that you have a hard time liking yourself. I ask you to tell me more about what it feels like to be the way you describe yourself. How did you reach these conclusions about your worth as a person?

I do not offer you immediate reassurance that indeed you are an adequate person who is likeable. Although reassuring feedback may make you feel good for a short time, it is doubtful that this feeling would be longlasting. Your internal critic will not believe any positive feedback I might offer you—at least if I attempt to reassure you too soon. I am more interested in assisting you in exploring both your feelings and your thoughts. I also want to give you a chance to express what you often don't say. If you are able to talk fully about feeling inadequate and having difficulty liking yourself, you stand a better chance of arriving at your own solutions to the problems you face. I strive to create a therapeutic climate that will enable you to sort out your thoughts and feelings, which will put you in a place to make better decisions and changes. Mere reassurance and advice do not facilitate self-examination, but a willingness to listen to you can encourage you to share what you are feeling in the moment, to engage in significant self-disclosure, and to explore your struggles.

Even though you may have stayed with some intense feelings and allowed yourself to experience the reverberations of your feelings in your body, you might well become uncomfortable and want to distance yourself from some feelings that arise as you talk with me. You may express fears about getting involved and display resistance toward any attempt at delving into deeply personal concerns. Assume you say: "I'm afraid that if I get deep into my feelings I'll get stuck in a quagmire and won't be able to get out. I'm afraid if I let myself feel that I'll get out of control. There is a part of me that wants to get into my emotions, yet another part of me wants to get into my head and keep control." Whether or not your fears are expressed, they tend to give rise to some ambivalence: the desire to reveal yourself is balanced by the reluctance to expose yourself. To work with your ambivalence, I suggest a role play in which we each take one of these two sides of yourself.

Gestalt therapy and psychodrama often employ an empty-chair or two-chair technique. This is another way to act out your present feelings in the therapy session. Having a dialogue with various aspects within yourself, or between yourself and another individual, is particularly useful when you are feeling ambivalent about a direction to pursue or when you are in a conflictual situation. I invite you not to talk about an issue but to make it present by actually bringing to life a conflict you are experiencing. For instance, imagine that you tell me that you often feel very young and awkward when you try to relate your accomplishments to your mother. I suggest to you: "So, sitting in the chair you are in now, become that young and awkward person and talk to this other (empty) chair—to your mother. What would you like your mother to know about your accomplishments? What are you saying to your mother in this scene?" Now switch chairs and become your mother and reply the way you expect her to—or reply in the manner that you would hope she would. By bringing emotionally laden material or a conflict into the present through this two-chair exercise, you and I get a better understanding of how you struggle with relationships or with feeling young and foolish. Experiential techniques adapted from psychodrama and Gestalt therapy tend to facilitate a deeper understanding and insight, as well as a greater emotional connection to your words.

An alternative way I might work with your feelings about your mother is to suggest that you participate in a soliloquy, another psychodrama technique. Imagine yourself in a place where you can think out loud (soliloquize) and say what you are thinking and feeling. This could be a useful follow-up intervention to the two-chair dialogue between you and your mother. This technique facilitates clarification and an open expression of what you may be experiencing internally but not expressing verbally.

Future projection, another psychodrama technique, is also designed to help you express and clarify concerns you have about your future. An anticipated event is brought into the present moment and acted out. In this case, you enact a version of the way you hope a situation will ideally unfold between you and your mother. Of course, you could enact a dreaded fear of tomorrow with the most horrible outcome. For instance, your mother might tell you that she does not expect you to ever accomplish anything of any merit. Once you clarify your hopes for a particular outcome, you are in a better position to take specific steps that will enable you to achieve the future you desire.*

WORKING WITH AN EMOTIVE FOCUS

Many clients avoid becoming more emotionally connected to their words and experiences. Out of self-protection, they may compartmentalize their emotions and attitudes, which leads to a damming up of emotions. In therapy, when clients are able to reconnect their emotions and bodily reactions to certain events in life, emotions tend to be released—tears, laughter, anger, vulnerability, guilt, hope. This is the catharsis that often accompanies the experiential aspect of therapy. If clients are given the opportunity to talk and if the therapist pays attention to what clients are communicating, this alone may be enough to trigger intense emotional reactions.

And why is emotional release even necessary? There is a connection between physical health and emotional health. Abundant research teaches us that many physical illnesses and psychosomatic symptoms are the result of bottling up emotions. If you swallow your anger, you pay a price for this. If you are chronically under intense stress, your body reacts with a

* For a more detailed discussion of other techniques I might employ with you in an emotionally focused manner, refer to Chapters 9 and 11 of this book and to Corey (2000, Chapter 8).

host of illnesses. If you hold in all of your emotional pain, you expend a great deal of energy, and this takes a toll on your body. Clearly there are links between repressing emotions and symptoms such as headaches, asthma, backaches, arthritis, and muscular tension. I am convinced that it takes a great deal of energy to deny emotional pain. Somehow denied emotions will be expressed in the body. That which is not given expression tends to linger in the background and clamors for closure. For example, if you are excessively blocked from your grief after a significant loss or death of someone you love, the result will be a chronic sense of pain. This unexpressed pain is likely to prevent you from being emotionally open to experiencing the fullness of other relationships.

Experiential techniques borrowed from psychodrama such as empty chair work, soliloquy, future projection, role reversal, and role playing can be a route to healing an emotional wound. If clients have blocked sadness and grief over losing a special person, either through death or the breakup of a relationship, this unexpressed pain tends to keep them stuck. It can also interfere with intimacy because they fear once again experiencing a loss. The catharsis that occurs in therapy is a release of pent-up feelings, which facilitates the healing process.

I don't think it is necessary to press for catharsis as an end goal, however. For some clients, expressing intense emotions may be contraindicated. Blatner (1985) points out that this emotional release occurs when the sense of self expands in any of four categories: abreaction when one rediscovers one's previously disowned feelings; renewed hope in discovering how those feelings can be integrated into one's life; relief that one's full being can be accepted; and a deepened sense of significance as one finds meaning in life. Although catharsis is a natural part of many of the experiential or emotionally focused therapies (especially Gestalt therapy, existential therapy, person-centered therapy, and psychodrama), it is not in itself a goal. Rather, it is an indicator of emotional expansion and integration. Blatner (1985) suggests that dramatic emotional releases should not become the exclusive focus in therapeutic work, for subtle and gentle catharses can also result in healing.

Insight, or gaining an increased awareness of a problem situation, often follows the process of an emotional release. Insight is the cognitive shift that connects the awareness of the various emotional experiences with some meaningful narrative or some growing understanding. Insight adds a degree of understanding to the catharsis and allows clients to begin the essential process of gaining control over inappropriate modes of either suppressing or expressing those feelings. Further, clients gradually come to a cognitive and emotional (or experiential) understanding that they no longer have to continue living as they did before.

Both Gestalt therapy and psychodrama frequently involve some form of catharsis. Although there is value in catharsis, my experience with therapy groups has taught me time and again how essential it is to provide a context in which clients can come to an understanding of how their bottled-up emotions have affected both themselves and their relationships. Yet emotional release and self-understanding alone do not seem sufficient to produce lasting changes in thinking, feeling, and behaving.

Integrating insights and developing and practicing more effective behaviors is cognitive work. Formulating action plans toward the end of a therapy session is often most effective. Take time to make a few comments about the process and determine what can be done to practice in daily life. One excellent way to help clients achieve closure on emotional issues is to have them begin to think about the meaning of their heightened emotional states. Encourage clients to formulate their own interpretations of their problem situations and to reflect on how their beliefs and decisions may be contributing to some of the emotional turmoil they are re-experiencing.

WORKING WITH RUTH IN IDENTIFYING AND EXPLORING FEELINGS

See Session 7 (Emotive Focus in Counseling) of the *Student Video and Workbook for the Art of Integrative Counseling.*

The person-centered approach stresses that one of the first stages in the therapy process involves identifying, clarifying, and learning how to express feelings. I encourage Ruth to talk about any feelings she is aware of, especially those that are a source of difficulty. These feelings are likely to be vague and difficult to identify at first.

One of Ruth's main therapeutic goals is for her to come to terms with her inner truths, which involves her having a better sense of what she thinks and feels. Greenberg, Rice, and Elliot (1993) describe the steps involved in the process of attaining this expanded awareness, which I will integrate in the discussion of my work with Ruth here.

The beginning of the process of facilitating Ruth's experiential emotional process is anchored on establishing a sense of safety in the therapy situation. If I can create a nonjudgmental and accepting environment, the chances are greatly increased that Ruth will eventually be able to unconditionally accept herself with all of her feelings. During the early stages of our sessions, I rely on listening with understanding. I encourage Ruth to talk about what most concerns her and what recent events have led to her decision to come to therapy at this time. Greenberg and her colleagues refer to this as encouraging "storytelling."

If I can really hear Ruth's deeper verbal and nonverbal messages, some of which may not be fully clear to her, I can respond to her in a way that lets her know that I have some appreciation for what it is like in her world. Grasping the subjective or experiential world of clients is a key concept of many theoretical orientations including existential therapy, Gestalt therapy, person-centered therapy, and Adlerian therapy. I need to do more than merely reflect what I hear her saying; I need to share with her my reactions as I listen to her. The more I am able to communicate that I understand and accept the feelings she has, the less need she has to deny or deflect her feelings. As a result, Ruth's capacity for clearly identifying what she is feeling at any moment gradually increases.

There is a great deal of value in letting Ruth tell her story in the way she chooses. The way she walks into the office, her gestures, her style of speech, the details she chooses to go into, and what she decides to relate and not to relate provide me with clues to her world. By being attentive and tracking what she is doing in the moment, I am getting a larger picture of her world. Certainly I am not getting the entire story, but it is possible to grasp significant samples of Ruth's story. At this time Ruth is giving me the "short version" of her life story. I will inquire about Ruth's presentation as a way to understand the personal meanings of her thoughts and feelings pertaining to events in her life. My interventions are aimed at checking to make sure that I am understanding her accurately and conveying to her my understanding of her situation. Here I am influenced by concepts from the person-centered approach such as listening with understanding, presence, and focusing on the subjective aspects of a client's experiencing.

If I do too much structuring too soon and if I am too directive, I will interfere with her typical style of presenting herself. So, at this early stage of counseling, I agree with the person-centered therapists who stress attending and listening on the counselor's part and who focus on the productive use of silence. Although I am not inclined to promote long silences early in counseling, there is value in not jumping in too soon when silences occur. Instead of coming to the rescue, it is better to explore the meanings of the silence.

To help Ruth express and explore her feelings, I draw heavily on Gestalt therapy experiments. I teach Ruth to pay attention to what is emerging in her awareness. I am guided by the shifts in her awareness, and together we create experiments that grow out of her present-centered awareness. The emphasis is on our dialogue and the quality of contact we are able to make in the therapy session. Because she has yet to work through her feelings of not feeling valued for who she is, such issues surface in her therapy. Ruth is aware that her value comes from the functions she performs for her family. She does not feel that she is valued apart from what she is able to do for others.

I invite Ruth to experience her feelings fully, instead of speculating about the reasons she behaves as she does. I ask her to bring whatever she is feeling into the present by reliving an event surrounding these feelings rather than by merely reporting outside events or long-standing themes in her life. For instance, if she says that she is sad when she thinks about how people in her family do not give her recognition in her own right, I ask that she stay with the sadness. If she can, I encourage her to share at this moment how she is experiencing her sadness. If she reports feeling tense, I ask her *how* she experiences this tension and *where* it is located in her body. I encourage Ruth to make contact with her feelings by asking her to "be that feeling." My rationale for doing this is based on my belief that direct experiencing is more therapeutic than talking about a feeling or event. Thus, if Ruth has a knot in her stomach, she can intensify her feeling of tension by "becoming the knot, giving it voice and personality." If I notice that she has moist eyes, I may direct her to "be her tears now." By putting words to her tears, she avoids merely abstractly intellectualizing about all the reasons *why* she is sad or tense. Before she can change her feelings, she must allow herself to *fully experience* these feelings. The experiential therapies give me valuable tools for guiding Ruth to the expression of feelings.

In this session I have made many different interventions, one of which is to ask Ruth to talk to me as her husband. I ask her to stay with whatever she is experiencing, paying particular attention to her body and to the emotions welling up in her, doing her best to express these emerging feelings. Role-playing Ruth's husband gives me an opportunity to observe how Ruth presents herself to her husband and to get some sense of how he might receive her verbal and nonverbal messages. For Ruth the role play is likely to trigger feelings surrounding a situation with her husband, which brings her work to a deeper level than if she had merely reported a situation.

Toward the end of an emotionally intense role-playing session, I suggest to Ruth that as homework she write a letter to her husband expressing some of the feelings that just came up for her. But I stress to her the importance of not giving him this letter—at least not now. Writing the letter may trigger memories, and Ruth may experience further emotional release. I hope this will help her begin thinking about the influence her husband has on her life. By writing the letter Ruth is likely to gain clarity and a new perspective on how she wants to approach her husband. Even if the letter is burned or buried after writing, this can be a very therapeutic exercise because Ruth is able to release feelings that have been kept under cover. At our next session I will ask Ruth if she wrote the letter, and, if she did, what it was like for her to do so. What was she feeling and thinking as she was writing to her husband? How was she affected when she read the letter later? Is there anything that she wants to share with me? The direction of our session could depend on her response as Ruth provides clues to where we need to go next.

CONCLUDING COMMENTS

I have emphasized the role of expressing feelings in the therapeutic process. Now let me give you a few guidelines for doing experiential, emotionally focused work with your clients. It is important for you to be able to experience your own emotions and to deal with them in a healthy way. Your ability to be emotionally present for your clients hinges on how centered you are yourself and whether you have access to your own emotions. If you are frightened of your feelings, you won't be able to facilitate a process with clients that enables them to express and work through their feelings. If you are scared of your own anger or of anger directed toward you, it will be quite difficult for you to assist clients in dealing constructively with their anger. If you have bottled up your own pain over significant losses, you will not be able to be present for clients as they open painful subjects in their therapy.

If you are extremely uncomfortable with conflict, it is unlikely that you will be instrumental in helping clients stay with a conflict long enough to bring resolution to a situation. If you are afraid that if you cry you will lose control, how can you expect to deal with clients who keep their tears inside lest they get hopelessly out of control? If your emotions frighten you, you will find some way to divert your clients' attention away from intense feelings. If a client is afraid of becoming engulfed in depression and you are running from depression, how are you going to be able to therapeutically engage this individual?

To assist your clients in managing their emotional life, you need to be managing your own emotions. As your clients relive painful memories attached to events, you must be able to care about them without getting lost in their emotional pain. If you are easily triggered by the emotionally laden stories of your clients, you may not have the objectivity to help them work through painful scenarios. As you will read in Chapter 10, clients are bound to open some of your old wounds. How you deal with this will determine how therapeutic you can be for your clients. If your clients affect you emotionally as they delve into intense emotions, be aware of the feelings this evokes in you. Recognize your own emotional reactions and put them on hold until you can be properly attended to in your own supervision or therapy sessions.

I have placed a great deal of importance on assisting clients in the process of identifying, experiencing, and exploring their emotions. However, this does not imply that you should insist that your clients always deal with their emotions. Begin where your client is, and determine what would be most useful for that client at that particular time. If you push too hard for emotional expression, or if you encourage clients to "get in contact with their feelings" too soon, clients are likely to become uncomfortable and defensive. Keep in mind that the emotional work needs to be connected with what clients are thinking and doing. It may serve little therapeutic purpose to elicit feelings from clients if this is done mainly for dramatic effect. You must not meet your needs as a therapist by manipulating your clients.

8

Behavioral Focus in Counseling

The term *behavior therapy* refers to the application of a diversity of techniques and procedures that are rooted in a variety of learning theories. No single theory undergirds the practice of contemporary behavior therapy, and there is no single form that this approach takes. My integrated behavioral focus includes standard (or traditional) behavior therapy along with other action-oriented therapies. These other related therapy systems include multimodal therapy, cognitive behavior therapy, rational emotive behavior therapy, cognitive therapy, and reality therapy. From an integrative perspective, I will be addressing some basic concepts that most of these theoretical orientations share and describing a range of behavioral techniques associated with these other action-oriented models.

The behavioral perspective is in contrast to the relationship-oriented and experiential approaches described in the previous chapter. Experiential approaches place considerable emphasis on clients' achieving insight into their problems as a prerequisite for change. Behavior therapists operate on the premise that changes in behavior can occur *prior* to understanding oneself and that behavioral changes may well lead to an increased level of self-understanding. I draw on a wide variety of behavioral techniques derived from social learning theory, such as reinforcement, modeling, shaping, cognitive restructuring, desensitization, relaxation training, coaching, and behavioral rehearsal. Indeed, behavioral interventions can be incorporated into many of the relationship-oriented therapies, and by doing so clients can consolidate their learning and continue to solve new problems as they arise.

The behaviorally oriented perspective I am describing in this chapter assists clients in exploring how past and present thoughts, feelings, and behaviors have worked for them and what they have cost. The action-oriented therapies provide methods that are measurable, plan-specific, and realistic. From an integrative perspective, a behavioral framework is most useful in the later stages of clients' work, after they have explored their feelings and identified and worked with underlying cognitions.

I particularly value the call for action typical of behavioral approaches because I believe such actions are necessary to bring about significant personal change.

BENEFITS AND LIMITATIONS OF A BEHAVIORAL FOCUS

From the behaviorally oriented models I especially appreciate the emphasis on specifics and the need for a systematic application of therapeutic techniques. Clients often make global statements such as "I feel unloved; life has no meaning." Behavioral approaches aim toward greater specificity so that focused therapy can proceed. A behavioral therapist might reply like this to such a global statement: "Who specifically is not loving you? What is going on in your life to bring about this meaninglessness? What are some specific things you might be doing that contribute to the state you are in? What would you most like to change?"

One of the major benefits of a behavioral focus is the wide variety of specific behavioral techniques available to me in counseling diverse client populations. Because the behavioral emphasis is on *doing,* as opposed to merely talking about problems and gathering insights, clients formulate plans of action for changing behavior. Behavioral interventions can be employed to treat a wide array of problems: helping people stick to an exercise plan, managing stress, and treating hypertension, to name a few. Perhaps most important of all is that behavioral strategies are well suited to an integrative approach because these methods can be incorporated into most of the other therapeutic systems. In fact, behavior therapy is at its best when it is used integratively. Clients who are looking for action plans and behavioral change are likely to cooperate with behavioral approaches because they include concrete methods for dealing with problems of living. In addition, a behavioral focus fits well with short-term counseling.

In zeroing in on the behavioral perspective, listen very carefully to your clients and allow them to express and explore their feelings before implementing a treatment plan. The basic therapeutic conditions stressed by the person-centered therapist—active listening, accurate empathy, positive regard, genuineness, respect, and immediacy—should be integrated into a behavioral framework. If you are too eager to work toward resolving problems, you may pay little attention to exploring feelings. There are pitfalls in focusing too tightly on clients' presenting problems instead of listening to the deeper message. Thus, if you are teaching clients assertion skills that they can use in a job interview, remain open to dealing with their thoughts (self-talk) associated with going to the interview as well as their emotional reactions (anxiety).

UNDERSTANDING THE SEVEN MODALITIES OF HUMAN FUNCTIONING

Assessment is a crucial step in using a behavioral approach to therapeutic change, and Arnold Lazarus has provided a useful way to obtain information and target personal goals. The essence of Lazarus's BASIC I.D. model is that the complex personality of humans can be divided into seven major areas of functioning: B = behavior; A = affective responses; S = sensations; I = images; C = cognitions; I = interpersonal relationships; and D = drugs, biological functions, nutrition, and exercise (Lazarus, 1989, 1992, 1995, 1997a, 1997b). Although these modalities are interactive, they can be considered discrete functions. Clients are social beings who move, feel, sense, imagine, and think. A comprehensive assessment of these seven modalities of human functioning is an important part of the behavioral approach.

The BASIC I.D. is the cognitive map that provides systematic attention to each aspect of human functioning. Let's take a closer look at each of the modalities in the BASIC I.D.

1. *Behavior.* This modality refers primarily to overt behaviors, including acts, habits, and reactions that are observable and measurable. Some questions asked are: "What would you like to change?" "What would you like to start doing?" "What would you like to stop doing?"
2. *Affect.* This modality refers to emotions, moods, and strong feelings. Questions asked include: "What emotions do you experience most often?" "What emotions are problematic for you?"
3. *Sensation.* This area refers to the five basic senses of touch, taste, smell, sight, and hearing. A typical question asked is: "Do you suffer from unpleasant sensations, such as pains, aches, dizziness, and so forth?"
4. *Imagery.* This modality pertains to ways in which we picture ourselves, and it includes memories, dreams, and fantasies. A few questions asked are: "How do you see yourself now?" "How would you like to be able to see yourself in the future?"
5. *Cognition.* This modality refers to insights, ideas, opinions, self-talk, and judgments that constitute one's fundamental values, attitudes, and beliefs. Questions include: "What are the values and beliefs you most cherish?" "What are some negative things you say to yourself?" "What are the main 'shoulds,' 'oughts,' and 'musts' in your life? How do they get in the way of effective living?"
6. *Interpersonal relationships.* This modality refers to interactions with other people. Examples of questions include: "What do you expect from the significant people in your life?" "What do they expect from you?" "Are there any relationships with others that you hope to change?"

7. *Drugs/biology.* This modality includes more than drugs; it takes into consideration one's nutritional habits and exercise patterns. Typical questions are: "Do you have any concerns about your health?" "Do you take any prescribed drugs?" "What are your habits pertaining to diet, exercise, and physical fitness?"

Once this initial assessment is complete, more focused discussions can proceed in identified problem areas. This leads to identification of therapy goals, the first step in a treatment plan.

BECOMING THE CLIENT: Experiencing Behaviorally Oriented Therapy

Put yourself in the role of the client as a way to experience the benefits of behaviorally oriented therapy. Self-awareness is a crucial step in the change process, yet insights without action will hardly move you forward. The behavioral methods described in this section can be most useful in translating your insights into concrete action plans.

As my client, it is very likely you will experience a diverse range of behavioral strategies. In addition to exploring your beliefs and thinking, along with exploring feelings associated with your thoughts, the behavioral perspective is essential. A place for us to start working is by doing a brief, but comprehensive, assessment using the BASIC I.D. model.

Once this initial assessment of the seven behavioral areas is completed, the next phase of work deals with problem areas and allows me to understand you more fully. We are then ready to identify a set of therapy goals that both of us mutually agree are suitable for your therapy. Which of these behavioral goals will you set for yourself?

- Learning to ask clearly and directly for what you want
- Learning to be assertive without becoming aggressive
- Acquiring habits that lead to physical and psychological relaxation
- Developing specific habits for a healthy lifestyle (exercising regularly, controlling eating patterns, reducing stress)
- Monitoring your behavior or cognitions as a means to change
- Being able to recognize and to challenge self-destructive thought patterns or critical self-statements that lead to problematic behaviors
- Learning communication and social skills
- Developing problem-solving strategies to cope with a variety of situations encountered in daily life

Once you have identified your goals, I will help you break down these general goals into specific, concrete, measurable goals that can be pursued in a systematic fashion. For example, if you say you'd like to feel more adequate in social situations, I ask: "What are you doing or not doing that seems to be related to your feeling of inadequacy? What are the conditions under which you feel inadequate? Can you give me some concrete examples of situations in which you feel inadequate? In what specific ways would you like to change your behavior?"

Borrowing from reality therapy, I find Wubbolding's (2000) WDEP formulation to be especially useful in my work with you.

- **W** stands for exploring wants, needs, and perceptions. I do not tell you what you should change but encourage you to examine what you want.
- **D** stands for exploring the direction of your current behavior and determining what you are doing to attain this.
- **E** stands for evaluation, which consists of you making your own evaluation about what you are actually doing. It is up to you to decide how well your current behavior is working for you.
- **P** stands for planning.

In applying reality therapy, much of what we do consists of developing realistic and specific plans and then talking about how you might carry them out in everyday life. Knowing what you are willing to change is the first step. Through self-evaluation you can determine what you have been doing that is not working. This lowers resistance and opens you up to other behaviors or directions. Knowing how to bring about this change is the next step. At each of these points in the WDEP model specific questions get you to look at what you are doing and figure out better ways to arrange your life.

After you and I work through the steps in the WDEP model and identify therapeutic goals, it is necessary to decide on the various avenues by which these goals can be accomplished. You may have trouble reaching your goals because your plans are not sufficiently thought out, which makes them difficult to implement. Once you know what you want, the next step is figuring out how to get it. By developing and assessing behavioral strategies together, we can move in the direction of making your vision a reality.

One of the aspects I particularly like about behavior therapy and related action therapies is the wide range of behavioral techniques I can employ in assisting you to move in the direction you desire. Here is a sample of the behavioral strategies we might apply as a route to meeting your personal goals:

- You indicate that you experience a good deal of anxiety. You find yourself racing and doing too many things at once. I teach you a few basic relaxation procedures that you agree to practice once a day.
- You say that you want to get better at asking for what you want, without sounding apologetic. I use strategies such as coaching, modeling, and assertion training to teach you how to approach others more effectively.
- You decide you want to improve in managing your time. You find that you procrastinate a great deal and then rush to complete projects. Together

we brainstorm possibilities for creatively dealing with procrastination. We come up with a number of specific points for better managing your time as a student: focus on demanding subjects first, set goals in number of pages of a reading assignment, create a reward system, avoid guilting yourself about what you don't do, give yourself credit for what you do, stop the interruptions, allow for short breaks.

■ You would like to reduce your anxiety when you feel you are being tested, which is preventing you from going on job interviews. I begin with a specific analysis of the nature of your anxiety by asking how you experience this anxiety in specific situations where you feel you "must perform," including what you actually *do* in these situations: "When did it begin? What are some situations when you most experience this anxiety? What do you do at these times? What are your feelings and thoughts in these situations? How do your present fears interfere with obtaining what you want? What are the consequences of your behaviors in threatening situations?" After this assessment, we define specific behavioral goals, and I introduce strategies to help you reduce your anxiety to a manageable level. For example, you state one of your goals as: "I will arrange for one job interview during this week and report back at our next session." I get a commitment from you to work toward this goal, as well as any others you agree to at later times, and together we evaluate your progress toward meeting these goals throughout the duration of therapy.

■ You are expected to actively work outside of your counseling sessions. At each of your sessions we collaboratively design homework activities that enable you to take into your daily life what you are learning in the office. Homework is carefully designed and is aimed at getting you to carry out positive actions and induce emotional and attitudinal change. This practice extends the value of the brief time we have during a session and fosters an active stance on your part in working on your goals. Toward the end of therapy, I encourage you to review your progress, make plans, and identify strategies for dealing with continuing or potential problems.

Going back to the multimodal BASIC I.D. assessment grid, you can now see how it is possible to have a behavioral orientation in a broad sense. Behavior includes emotions, sensations, imagery, cognition, interpersonal relationships, and health. Because you are an integrated being functioning in all of these modalities, a behavioral focus in counseling must attend to more than simply what you are doing. Your thoughts, feelings, and physiological reactions influence your behaving. As we work on specific behaviors that we have targeted for exploration, I also need to be mindful of thoughts and feelings you are experiencing pertaining to the behavioral dimension.

Throughout our work together, I will encourage you to see the value in actively trying new behavior rather than being passive and leaving action to chance. One way of fostering an active stance is to formulate clear contracts, including writing out a plan of action. In this way you are continually being confronted with what you want and what you are willing to do.

DEVELOPING A BEHAVIORAL CONTRACT

Contracts are a useful frame of reference for evaluating the outcomes of counseling, but designing a behavioral contract is not as easy as it may seem. In the planning phase I borrow some specific aspects of formulating and carrying out a plan that I have adapted from a prominent reality therapist, Robert Wubbolding (2000). Here are some specific suggestions for creating an effective plan.

- Plans are based on your personal goals. Begin by having clients specify what changes they desire. Goals should be measurable, attainable, positive, and significant to clients.
- Goals must be translated into target behaviors. Ask clients what specific behaviors they want to increase or decrease. Design plans around the answer to this question.
- After clients make the evaluation of behavioral changes they want to acquire, an action program to bring about change is devised.
- Encourage clients to come up with clear plans for what they will do today, tomorrow, and the next day to bring about change and to anticipate what might get in the way of their plans.
- It is a good idea to begin the plan as soon as possible. Ask clients "What are you willing to do today to begin to change your life?" "What are you going to do now to attain your stated goals?"
- Good plans are simple and easy to understand. Plans should be flexible and open to modification as clients gain a deeper understanding of the specific behaviors they want to change.
- The plan should be within the limits of clients' motivation and capacities. Like goals, plans should be realistic, attainable, and reflective of what clients need and want.
- Good plans are specific. Develop specificity by addressing questions such as "What?" "Where?" "With whom?" "When?" and "How often?"
- Plans are best stated in positive terms by pointing out what will be done rather than what won't be done.
- It is a good idea to develop plans clients can carry out by themselves. Plans that are contingent on what others will do or not do can be restrictive.
- In choosing action-oriented steps, it is essential that clients consider their internal and external resources and limitations.
- Effective plans are repetitive and ideally are performed daily.

- Effective planning involves process-centered activities, such as applying for a job, writing a letter to a friend, taking a yoga class, devoting two hours a week to volunteer work, or taking a vacation.
- It may be necessary to revise the plan from time to time. Ask the client, "Is your plan helpful?" If the plan does not work, it can be reevaluated and alternatives considered.

Creating and carrying out behavioral plans enables clients to gain effective control over their lives. This is clearly the teaching phase of counseling, which is best directed toward providing clients with new information and assisting them in the discovery of more effective ways of getting what they want and need.

Resolutions and plans are empty unless there is a decision to carry them out. It is crucial that clients commit to a definite plan that they can realistically accomplish. The ultimate responsibility for making plans and implementing them rests with clients. Clients are learning specific skills with the expectation that they will be responsible for transferring what they learn in the counseling setting to everyday life. In behavior therapy, clients are expected to engage in specific actions to deal with their problems. My goal is to consistently encourage clients to learn specific information and skills for coping with a range of challenges they will encounter in day-to-day living. The expectation is that clients can become their own counselor by learning a set of skills for effective living that they can apply not only to present problems but also to future difficulties.*

BEHAVIORAL FOCUS WITH RUTH

See Session 8 (Behavioral Focus in Counseling) of the *Student Video and Workbook for the Art of Integrative Counseling.*

My initial focus is on doing a thorough assessment of Ruth's current behavior. I use the BASIC I.D. model to obtain useful information and target personal goals.†

I ask Ruth to monitor what she is doing so that we can create baseline data to evaluate any changes. We then continue our work by collaboratively developing concrete goals. I draw on a wide range of cognitive and behavioral techniques to help Ruth achieve her goals, including stress-reduction techniques, assertion training, behavior rehearsals, modeling, coaching, systematic desensitization, in vivo desensitization, flooding, and relaxation

---

* For further discussion of behavior therapy and other action-oriented approaches, see Corey (2001c, Chapter 10), Corsini and Wedding (1995, Chapter 7), Lazarus (1997a), Prochaska and Norcross (1999, Chapter 9), Sharf (2000, Chapter 8), and Wubbolding (2000).

† For a detailed description of a multimodal-behavior therapist's perspective on Ruth by Arnold Lazarus, see *Case Approach to Counseling and Psychotherapy* (Corey, 2001b, Chapter 8).

methods. I emphasize learning new coping behaviors that Ruth can use in everyday situations. She practices these activities both during her therapy sessions and during the week outside of the office.*

How do Ruth and I determine the degree to which she is progressing? What criteria do we use to make this determination? Behavioral interventions have measurable results. Techniques must be continually verified to determine how well they are working. Behavior changes in Ruth are a major basis for making this evaluation. Her own evaluation of how much progress she sees and how satisfied she is by the outcomes is a major factor in assessing therapeutic results.

In a particular counseling session Ruth tells me that she feels encouraged to go forward and make some of the changes that are important to her. She brings up the subject of her weight. As we talk about what her weight means to her, Ruth mentions that she does not exercise and that she does not have much energy. I need to be careful not to make a decision for Ruth regarding developing an exercise program and managing her weight. Instead, it is critical to ascertain what Ruth wants in these areas. Although I am utilizing behavioral strategies with Ruth, I also employ techniques from feminist therapy such as gender-role analysis and gender-role intervention. This involves asking Ruth to recall parental messages she received related to weight and appearance. The technique of gender-role intervention places Ruth's concern about her weight in the context of society's role expectations for women. My aim is to provide Ruth with insight into the ways social issues and unrealistic standards of the "perfect body" are affecting her psychologically. This leads to a discussion of unrealistic strivings that Ruth has bought into and a critical appraisal of how she measures her worth.

After discussing which messages Ruth wants to change, we implement a plan for creating these changes. Ruth states that she does want to develop a regular exercise program. If Ruth's program is to work well for her, she must identify what type of exercise is appropriate for her. Once she is clear that she wants to commit herself to regular exercise, we are ready to formulate an action plan that will help her get what she wants. Together we determine that walking will be a vital part of her exercise program. We work out the details, including how often she will walk and for how long. I encourage her to use her friend as a source of support in helping her stick with her plans. Furthermore, I strongly recommend that Ruth find ways to monitor her progress and keep herself accountable to following her plans for appropriate eating and exercising habits.

Working from an integrative perspective, it is imperative that I also attend to Ruth's thoughts and feelings about her weight and her body image in general. Ruth has self-talk that is not helpful to her in this area. She badgers herself about not looking right and about being weak because she is overweight, giving herself negative messages. Ruth's negative self-talk

---

* For a fuller discussion of behavioral techniques, see Corey (2001c, Chapter 10).

leads to feelings of being defeated, overwhelmed, depressed, and angry with herself. When she tries to get into some of her clothes and they don't fit, she tells herself she is totally unattractive and feels upset and discouraged. It will not be enough to simply chart out the steps in a behavioral program for weight control through exercise and dieting. We will also need to address her thoughts and emotions at the same time as we are working behaviorally. Placing Ruth's concerns about her body in the context of societal standards that dictate what constitutes the ideal physical appearance may aid in Ruth's understanding. Because Ruth's concerns involve her thoughts, feelings, and actions, it is necessary to work on all these levels to some extent, even though we may focus on one particular dimension at certain times in counseling.

CONCLUDING COMMENTS

I recommend that you review the key themes of the behavioral approaches described in this chapter and apply them to yourself. Select at least one behavior you would like to change. Apply the WDEP model (of reality therapy) to identify a behavior you are willing to change. What is one of your behaviors that is not working for you at this time? This might be a behavior you'd like to reduce or a behavior that you'd like to acquire. Once you have selected your target behavior, apply the guidelines for developing an action plan to yourself. After reflecting on the personal applications, ask yourself what you'd want to incorporate from this approach as a counselor. How do you imagine it would be for you to be a client in behaviorally oriented therapy? What concepts and techniques from behavioral approaches most fit into your personal philosophy of counseling?

9

An Integrative Perspective

An integrative approach to counseling and psychotherapy is best characterized by attempts to look beyond and across the confines of single-school approaches to see what can be learned and how clients can benefit from other perspectives (Arkowitz, 1997). Integrative counseling is the process of selecting concepts and methods from a variety of systems. Ideally the integrative approach is a creative synthesis of the unique contributions of diverse theoretical orientations, dynamically integrating concepts and techniques that fit the uniqueness of your personality and style.

There are multiple pathways to achieving this integration, two of the most common being technical eclecticism and theoretical integration. *Technical eclecticism* tends to focus on differences, chooses from many approaches, and is a collection of techniques. This path calls for using techniques from different schools without necessarily subscribing to the theoretical positions that spawned them. In contrast, *theoretical integration* refers to a conceptual or theoretical creation beyond a mere blending of techniques. This path has the goal of producing a conceptual framework that synthesizes the best of two or more theoretical approaches to produce an outcome richer than that of a single theory (Norcross & Newman, 1992).

Arnold Lazarus (1997a), founder of multimodal therapy, espouses technical (or systematic) eclecticism. Multimodal therapists borrow from many other therapy systems, using techniques that have been demonstrated to be effective in dealing with specific problems. Lazarus raises concerns about theoretical eclecticism because he believes blending bits and pieces of different theories is likely to obfuscate matters. He contends that by remaining theoretically consistent but technically eclectic practitioners can spell out precisely what interventions they will employ with various clients, as well as the means by which they select these procedures.*

* For a more detailed discussion of technical eclecticism, see Lazarus (1992, 1995, 1996b).

I see many advantages to incorporating a diverse range of techniques from many different theories, but I think it is also possible to incorporate key principles and concepts from various theoretical orientations. Some concepts from the experiential approaches blend quite well with cognitive behavioral approaches. For example, the experiential approaches emphasize here-and-now awareness, the therapeutic relationship, and an exploration of feelings—all concepts easily incorporated into action-oriented therapies. Clients can be asked to decide what they want to do with present awareness, including making behavioral plans for change. All the action-oriented therapies depend on a good rapport between client and therapist. Techniques will not take root if there is not a good working relationship, and clients are more likely to cooperate with a therapist's cognitive and behavioral interventions if they feel the therapist is genuinely interested in their welfare.

SEARCHING FOR COMMON DENOMINATORS ACROSS THERAPY SCHOOLS

The experiential approaches (such as existential therapy and Gestalt therapy) place a premium on exploration of feelings in the counseling process. However, the concept of working with feelings can certainly be linked closely with the necessity of exploring the thoughts and behaviors connected to these feelings. In short, the kind of eclecticism I am suggesting looks for common denominators across therapeutic schools. This involves identifying core concepts that different theories share or concepts that can be usefully combined. However, a word of caution is in order. Blending theoretical constructs is more challenging than utilizing diverse techniques from different schools. If you attempt to blend theoretical constructs from different orientations in your own integrative model, be sure that these concepts are indeed compatible. Some blending simply does not make much conceptual sense. For instance, psychodynamic theory, which focuses on unconscious factors as the source of present-day problems, does not blend nicely with theories that reject the unconscious (rational emotive behavior therapy and reality therapy). Likewise, psychodynamic theories are geared around central concepts such as exploration of past traumatic events, exploration of dreams, and working through the transference relationship. The theoretical models of rational emotive behavior therapy, behavior therapy, and reality therapy do not allow much room to explore these theoretical constructs. When blending different theoretical frameworks together, it is essential that these frameworks lend themselves to a fruitful merger.*

---

* Many textbooks in counseling theory have a chapter on integration of therapies. I recommend Abernethy (1992); Arkowitz (1997); Corey (2001c, Chapters 14 and 15); Gilliland and James (1998, Chapter 13); Ivey, Ivey, and Simek-Morgan (1997, Chapter 13); Patterson and Watkins (1996, Chapter 16); Prochaska and Norcross (1999, Chapters 14 and 15); and Sharf (2000, Chapter 15). Reading these survey chapters will give you a sense of the direction being taken by the psychotherapy integration movement.

THE BENEFITS AND LIMITATIONS OF INTEGRATION

Effective counseling involves proficiency in a combination of cognitive, affective, and behavioral techniques. Such a combination is necessary to help clients *think* about their beliefs and assumptions, to experience on a *feeling* level their conflicts and struggles, and to actually translate their insights into *action* programs by behaving in new ways in day-to-day living.

Preston (1998) contends that no one theoretical model can adequately address the wide range of problems clients will present in therapy. He says it is essential for therapists to have a basic grasp of various therapeutic models and for them to have at their disposal a number of intervention strategies. For Preston, the pivotal assessment question is, "What does this particular person most need in order to suffer less, to heal, to grow, or to cope more effectively?" Preston recommends that your selection of interventions be guided by your assessment of the client. This lends weight to the concept of integrating assessment with treatment, which I addressed in Chapter 8. Once you know what your client's target problems and goals are, it makes sense to design specific techniques tailor-made to your client.

Because I believe it is needlessly restrictive to apply only a few techniques from a single theory to most clients, I incorporate a wide range of procedures in my therapeutic style. However, unless you have an accurate, in-depth knowledge of theories, you cannot formulate a true synthesis. Simply put, you cannot integrate what you do not know (Norcross & Newman, 1992). Constructing your integrative orientation to counseling practice is a long-term venture that is refined with experience. Synthesizing various techniques or approaches in a systematic way is not accomplished merely by completing an introductory course in counseling theory. The challenge is for you to think and practice integratively—but critically.

There are some drawbacks to encouraging the development of an integrative model, as opposed to sticking primarily with one theory. I agree with those who are critical of a sloppy and internally inconsistent eclectic approach that is reduced to a random borrowing of ideas and techniques. At its worst, eclecticism can be an excuse for sloppy practice—a practice that lacks a systematic rationale for what you actually do in your work. If you merely pick and choose according to whims, it is likely that what you select will be just a reflection of your biases and preconceived ideas. It is important to avoid the trap of emerging with a hodgepodge of unamalgamated theories thrown hastily together.

DRAWING ON TECHNIQUES FROM VARIOUS THEORETICAL MODELS

For those of you who are beginning your counseling career, my general suggestion is to select the primary theory closest to your basic beliefs. Learn that theory as thoroughly as you can, and at the same time be open to discovering ways of drawing on techniques from many different theories. If you begin by working within the parameters of a single theory, you will have an anchor point from which to construct your own counseling perspective. But do not think that simply because you adhere to one theory you can use the same techniques with all of your clients. Even if you adhere to a single theory, you will need to be flexible in the manner in which you apply the techniques that flow from this theory as you work with different clients.

On this topic I am reminded of Paul's (1967) question: "*What* treatment, by *whom*, is the most effective *for this* individual with *that* specific problem, and under *what* set of circumstances?" Regardless of what model you may be working with, you must decide *what* techniques, procedures, or intervention methods to utilize, *when* to use them, and with *which* clients. This guideline is particularly true when you consider the reality that you will most likely encounter a diverse range of client populations. Do not become wedded to a favorite set of techniques that you apply in random fashion to all clients. Remember that the purpose of using techniques is to enhance your clients' explorations.

For counseling to be effective, it is necessary to utilize techniques and procedures in a manner that is consistent with clients' values, life experiences, and cultural background. Although it is unwise to stereotype clients because of their cultural heritage, it is useful to assess how the cultural context has a bearing on their problems. Some techniques may be contraindicated because of clients' socialization. Thus, clients' responsiveness (or lack of it) to certain techniques is a critical barometer in judging the effectiveness of these methods.

THE FOUNDATION OF MY INTEGRATIVE APPROACH

In this section I want to present some elements of my integrative approach to counseling. Existential theory comes closest to my worldview and serves as the foundation for constructing my theoretical orientation, but I also use two related theories extensively, Gestalt therapy and psychodrama. After briefly describing some of the key concepts and themes from the existential, Gestalt, and psychodrama orientations, I will show how I incorporate basic concepts and techniques from a number of the action-oriented therapies as well.

Existential Therapy as a Philosophical Base

My own philosophical orientation is strongly influenced by the existential approach, which conceives of counseling as a life-changing process. Counseling is a journey in which the therapist is a guide who facilitates client exploration. A number of key themes from the existential approach seem to me to capture the essence of the therapeutic venture. According to the existentialist view, we are capable of self-awareness, which is the distinctive capacity that allows us to reflect and to decide. With this awareness we become free beings who are responsible for choosing the way we live, and thus we influence our own destiny. I like the emphasis on freedom and responsibility, for this notion allows us to redesign our lives. I challenge people to look at the choices they *do* have, however limited they may be, and to accept responsibility for choosing for themselves. However, making choices gives rise to existential anxiety, which is another basic human characteristic. This anxiety is heightened when we reflect on the reality that we will die. Facing the inevitable prospect of eventual death gives the present moment significance as we become aware that we do not have forever to accomplish our projects. The reality of death is a catalyst that can lead to creating a life that has meaning and purpose. We strive toward a meaningful life by recognizing our freedom and by making a commitment to choose in the face of uncertainty.

Both existential therapy and person-centered therapy place central prominence on the person-to-person relationship. Client growth occurs through this genuine encounter. In my judgment, emphasizing the human quality of the therapeutic relationship lessens the chances of making counseling a mechanical process. In thinking about therapy from an existential perspective, I am not preoccupied with which techniques I might employ or with creating an agenda for my client. It is not the techniques I use that make a therapeutic difference; rather, it is the quality of my relationship with my client that heals. My main interests are in being as fully present as I am able to be for the client, establishing a trusting relationship, and moving into the client's subjective world. If my client is able to sense my presence and my desire to make a real connection, then a solid foundation is being created for the hard work that counseling entails.

Because the existential approach is concerned with the goals of therapy, basic conditions of human existence, and therapy as a shared journey, I do not feel bound by a specific set of techniques. Although I do incorporate a wide range of techniques from other orientations, my interventions are guided by a philosophical framework about the meaning of human existence. An existential view provides me with the framework for understanding universal human concerns, including facing and dealing with the problem of personal freedom, self-alienation and estrangement from others, the fear of death and nonbeing, living with courage, exploring the meaning of life, and making critical choices.

Existential therapy is really a philosophical approach that influences my practice. It is not a distinct or well-organized counseling model. In fact, the founders of existential therapy did not aim to create a separate school of therapy; they hoped its key concepts and themes would become integrated into all therapeutic schools (May & Yalom, 1995). Bugental and Bracke (1992) see the possibility of a creative integration of the conceptual propositions of existential therapy with psychodynamic or cognitive approaches. They indicate that experienced clinicians of contrasting orientations often accept some existential concepts and thus operate implicitly within an existential framework.*

---

* For further discussion of existential therapy, see Corey (2001c, Chapter 6), Corsini and Wedding (1995, Chapter 9), Prochaska and Norcross (1999, Chapter 4), and Sharf (2000, Chapter 5).

Gestalt Therapy: A Holistic Perspective

Gestalt therapy is truly an integrative orientation in that it focuses on whatever is in the client's awareness. From the Gestalt perspective, feelings, thoughts, body sensations, and actions are all used as guides to understand what is central for the client in each moment. The centrality of whatever is in the client's awareness is an ideal way to understand the world of the client. I attempt to approach clients without a preconceived set of biases or a set agenda. Instead, I place emphasis on what occurs phenomenologically with my client. By paying attention to the obvious verbal and nonverbal leads provided, I have a starting point for exploring the client's world.

Functioning within a Gestalt framework, I view my main goal as being to increase the client's awareness of "what is." Change occurs through a heightened awareness of what the client is experiencing moment to moment. The approach stresses present awareness and the quality of contact between the individual and the environment. Instead of trying to make something happen, my role is assisting the client to increase awareness, which will allow re-identification with the disowned parts of the self.

The Gestalt approach is characterized by many key concepts that can be fruitfully blended into other orientations. Gestalt therapy (and psychodrama) techniques allow clients to bring painful memories and feelings pertaining to both past and present events to center stage. Through the skillful and sensitive use of Gestalt therapy interventions, it is possible to assist clients in heightening their present-centered awareness of what they are thinking and feeling as well as what they are doing. The client is provided with a wide range of tools, in the form of Gestalt experiments, for making decisions about changing the course of living.

Gestalt therapy is a creative approach that utilizes the experiment to move clients from talk to action and experience. This is a perspective on growth and enhancement, not merely a system of techniques to treat disorders. With the emphasis given to the relationship between client and therapist, there is a creative spirit of suggesting, inventing, and carrying out experiments aimed at increasing awareness.*

Psychodrama: An Integrative Approach

Although psychodrama is primarily used in group therapy, many psychodrama techniques can be used fruitfully in individual counseling. Using psychodrama, the client acts out or dramatizes past, present, or anticipated life situations and roles. This is done in an attempt to gain deeper understanding, explore feelings and achieve emotional release, and develop be-

* For specific examples of Gestalt experiments when working with the emotive dimension, review Chapter 7. For further discussion of Gestalt therapy, see Corey (2001c, Chapter 8), Prochaska and Norcross (1999, Chapter 6), and Sharf (2000, Chapter 7).

havioral skills. Significant events are enacted to help the client get in contact with unrecognized and unexpressed feelings, to provide a channel for the full expression of these feelings and attitudes, and to broaden the role repertoire.

Integrated with other systems—such as psychodynamic, experiential, and cognitive behavioral approaches—psychodrama offers a more experiential process, adding imagery, action, and direct interpersonal encounter. In turn, psychodrama can utilize methods derived from the other experiential approaches and the cognitive behavioral approaches to ground clients in a meaningful process.

According to Blatner (1996), a major contribution of psychodrama is that it supports the growing trend toward technical eclecticism in psychotherapy. Practitioners are challenged to draw on whatever tools will be useful in a given situation. Yet psychodrama is best viewed as an optional set of tools rather than a single approach for all clients (Blatner, 1996). Psychodrama uses a number of specific techniques designed to intensify feelings, clarify implicit belief, increase self-awareness, and practice new behaviors. One of the most powerful tools of psychodrama is role reversal, which involves the client taking on the part of another person. Through reversing roles with a significant person, the client is able to formulate significant emotional and cognitive insights into his or her part in a relationship. This technique also creates empathy for the position of the other person. Variations of role playing and role reversal have many uses in both individual and group counseling. A few other techniques of psychodrama that I often utilize include self-presentation, soliloquy, coaching, modeling, role training, behavior rehearsal, and future projection.

It is clear that psychodramatic techniques can be adapted to fit well within the framework of many contemporary theoretical models, including psychoanalytic therapy, behavior therapies, multimodal therapy, Gestalt therapy, Adlerian therapy, play therapy, imagination therapy, Jungian therapy, family therapy, and group therapy. According to Blatner (1997), psychodrama's value lies in the fact that its methodology can be integrated with other therapeutic approaches rather than acting in seeming competition.*

DRAWING ON THE ACTION-ORIENTED THERAPIES

As much as I value working with the emotional realm, I find it essential to incorporate concepts and techniques from the action-oriented approaches to bring about both cognitive and behavioral changes. Here are a few of the ways I utilize the action-oriented therapies in my integrative model.

---

* See Blatner (1996 and 1997) and Corey (2000, Chapter 8) for a discussion of psychodrama applied to group counseling.

Behavior Therapy

A basic assumption of the behavioral perspective is that most problematic cognitions, emotions, and behaviors have been learned and that new learning can modify them. Although this modification process is often called "therapy," it is more properly an educational experience in which individuals are involved in a teaching/learning process. There are many parallels between counseling and education. Counseling is educational in that people develop a new perspective on ways of learning, and they also try out more effective ways of changing their cognitions, emotions, and behaviors. Many of the techniques employed by other action-oriented approaches with a strong behavioral core (such as rational emotive behavior therapy, cognitive therapy, reality therapy, and feminist therapy) share this basic assumption of counseling as an educational process. They stress the teaching/learning aspect of the counseling process. Techniques from the action-oriented approaches can be used to attain humanistic goals that characterize the experiential therapies. It is clear that bridges can connect experiential and behavior therapies.*

Multimodal Therapy

Multimodal therapy is a branch of behavior therapy. As you learned in Chapter 8, it is a comprehensive, systematic, holistic approach to behavior therapy developed by Arnold Lazarus (1989, 1995, 1997a). Grounding his practice on social learning theory, Lazarus endorses drawing techniques from just about all of the therapy models. In his integrative model new techniques are constantly being introduced and existing techniques are refined, but they are never used in a shotgun manner.

I selectively incorporate many multimodal concepts and strategies in my personal integrative style of counseling. Multimodal methods allow me to challenge self-defeating beliefs, offer constructive feedback, and provide positive reinforcement. I am able to coach, train, and model for my clients. Using this approach, I can function actively and directively by providing information and instruction. I am constantly adjusting my techniques to achieve the client's goals in therapy. I ask the question, "What is best for this particular person?" I make a careful attempt to determine precisely what relationship and what treatment strategies will work best with each client and under which particular circumstances. Because individuals are troubled by a variety of specific problems, it is appropriate that both a multitude of treatment strategies and different therapeutic styles are used to bring about change. Therapeutic flexibility and versatility, along with breadth over depth, are valued highly in the multimodal orientation.†

---

* For further discussion of behavior therapy, see Corey (2001c, Chapter 10), Corey (2000, Chapter 13), Corsini and Wedding (1995, Chapter 7), Prochaska and Norcross (1999, Chapter 9), and Sharf (2000, Chapter 8).

† For further discussion of multimodal therapy, see Corey (2001b, Chapter 8; 2001c, Chapter 10), Corsini and Wedding (1995, Chapter 11), and Lazarus (1997a).

Cognitive Behavior Therapy

Most of the contemporary therapies can be considered "cognitive" in a general sense because they have the aim of changing clients' subjective views of themselves and the world. However, the cognitive behavioral approaches differ from both psychodynamic and experiential therapies in that the major focus of cognitive behavior therapy (CBT) is on both undermining faulty assumptions and beliefs and teaching clients the coping skills needed to deal with their problems.

In many respects rational emotive behavior therapy (REBT) can be considered as a comprehensive and eclectic therapeutic practice. Numerous cognitive, emotive, and behavioral techniques can be employed in changing one's emotions and behaviors by changing the structure of one's cognitions. Further, REBT is open to using therapeutic procedures derived from other schools, especially from behavior therapy.

Beck's cognitive therapy is truly an integrative approach, drawing on many different modalities of psychotherapy (Alford & Beck, 1997). Cognitive therapy serves as a bridge between psychoanalytic therapy and behavior therapy. Cognitive therapy provides a structured, focused, active approach. It shares the phenomenological perspective of dealing with the client's inner world with Adlerian, existential, person-centered, psychodrama, and Gestalt therapies.

A feature I particularly value in all the cognitive behavioral therapies (and in feminist therapy) is the demystification of the therapy process. Being based on an educational model, these approaches all emphasize a working alliance between therapist and client. These approaches encourage self-help, provide for continuous feedback from the client on how well treatment strategies are working, and provide a structure and direction to the therapy process that allows for evaluation of outcomes. I especially appreciate the reality that clients are active, informed, and responsible for the direction of therapy because they are partners in the enterprise.*

Reality Therapy

In many ways choice theory, which underlies the practice of reality therapy, is grounded on phenomenological and existential premises. From the perspective of choice theory, we choose our goals and are responsible for the kind of world we create for ourselves. We are not helpless victims, and we can create a better life. We are responsible for what we choose to do, no matter what has happened in the past. Reality therapy shares many concepts with the cognitive behavioral therapies.

* For further discussion of cognitive behavior therapy and feminist therapy, see Corey (2001c, Chapters 11 and 12), Corey (2000, Chapter 14), Corsini and Wedding (1995, Chapters 6 & 8), Glasser (1998, 2000), Prochaska and Norcross (1999, Chapter 10), and Sharf (2000, Chapters 9, 10, & 12).

One concept of reality therapy that I find particularly useful is *total behavior,* which teaches that all behavior is made up of four inseparable but distinct components: *acting, thinking, feeling,* and the *physiology* that must accompany all of our actions, thoughts, and feelings. The main emphasis is given to acting and thinking, for these aspects of total behavior are easier to change than are the feeling and physiology components. The key to changing a total behavior lies in choosing to change what we are *doing* and *thinking,* for these are the behaviors that we can control. If we markedly change the doing and thinking component, the feeling and physiological components will change as well (Glasser, 1998, 2000).

I value the basic notion of the need to assume personal responsibility for our feelings that is stressed by reality therapy. This philosophy takes us out of a passive role and challenges us to accept our part in actually creating our feelings. For example, depression is not something that simply happens to us but is often a result of what we are doing and how we are thinking. Glasser (1998, 2000) speaks of "depressing" or "angering" rather than "being depressed" or "being angry." With this perspective, depression can be explained as an active choice we make rather than the result of being a passive victim. This process of "depressing" keeps anger in check, and it also allows us to ask for help. The use of the "ing" words serves to emphasize that feelings are behaviors, which are generated. Clearly, the emphasis of this theory is on how we act and think, and in this sense, it shares many of the themes of cognitive behavioral approaches.*

Adlerian Therapy

The basic goal of the Adlerian approach is to help clients identify and change their mistaken beliefs about self, others, and life and thus participate more fully in a social world. The therapeutic process helps clients make some basic changes in their style of living, which lead to changes in the way they feel and behave. I especially like the Adlerian perspective on therapy as a cooperative venture. Therapy is geared toward challenging clients to translate their insights into action in the real world.

One of the strengths of the Adlerian approach is its relationship to technical eclecticism. The Alderian model lends itself to versatility in meeting the needs of a diverse range of clients (Watts, 1999). Adlerians are not bound to follow a specific set of procedures, which gives them a great deal of freedom in working with clients. Adlerian therapists are resourceful in drawing on a variety of cognitive, behavioral, and experiential techniques that they think will work best for a particular client.

One of Adler's most important contributions is his influence on other therapy systems. Many of his basic ideas have found their way into other psychological schools, such as family systems approaches, Gestalt therapy, learning

* For further discussion of reality therapy and choice theory, see Corey (2001c, Chapter 9), Corey (2000, Chapter 15), Corsini and Wedding (1995, Chapter 10), Sharf (2000, Chapter 11), and Watts and Carlson (1999).

theory, reality therapy, rational emotive behavior therapy, cognitive therapy, person-centered therapy, and existentialism (Corey, as cited in Nystul, 1999a). All these approaches are based on a similar concept of the person as purposive and self-determining and as striving for growth and meaning in life.

The Adlerian perspective is holistic, meaning that individuals can be understood by taking into consideration all the aspects of human functioning. This theory addresses the client's past, present, and future. The notion of teleology, or striving for meaning and purpose, is central. I appreciate that this theory makes room to address spiritual concerns in counseling. The concept of social interest—that we need to contribute to making the world a better place—can be the foundation of any theoretical system. Going beyond the self and getting involved in making a difference in the lives of others is integrative in its very nature. All of these concepts can be incorporated in any theoretical model.

Contemporary Adlerian theory is an integration of cognitive, psychodynamic, and systems perspectives, and in many respects it resembles the social constructionist theories. Contemporary social constructionist theories, or constructivist therapies, share common ground with the Adlerian approach. Some of these common characteristics include an emphasis on establishing a respectful client/therapist relationship, an emphasis on clients' strengths and resources, and an optimistic and future orientation (Watts, 1999; Watts & Carlson, 1999).*

Feminist and Systemic Therapies

Feminist therapy is generally relatively short-term therapy aimed at both individual and social change. The major goal is to replace the current patriarchal system with feminist consciousness and thus create a society that values equality in relationships, that stresses interdependence rather than dependence, and that encourages women to define themselves rather than being defined by societal demands.

Feminist therapists are committed to actively breaking down the hierarchy of power in the therapeutic relationship through the use of various interventions. Some of these strategies are unique to feminist therapy, such as gender-role analysis and intervention, power analysis and intervention, assuming a stance of advocate in challenging conventional attitudes toward appropriate roles for women, and encouraging clients to take social action. Therapists with a feminist orientation understand how important it is to become aware of typical gender-role messages clients have been socialized with, and they are skilled in helping clients identify and challenge these messages. Feminist therapists also borrow therapeutic strategies from various therapy models. A few of these interventions include role playing, bibliotherapy, assertiveness training, behavior rehearsal, cognitive restructuring,

---

* For further discussion of Adlerian therapy, see Corey (2001c, Chapter 5), Corey, (2000, Chapter 7), Corsini and Wedding (1995, Chapter 3), Prochaska and Norcross (1999, Chapter 3), and Sharf (2000, Chapter 4).

psychodramatic techniques, identifying and challenging untested beliefs, and journal writing. Feminist therapy principles and techniques can be applied to a range of therapeutic modalities such as individual therapy, couples counseling, family therapy, group counseling, and community intervention.

Both feminist and systemic therapies are based on the assumption that individuals are best understood within the context of relationships. Most of the individual counseling theories do not place a primary focus on the role of systemic factors in influencing the individual. However, both feminist and systemic therapies operate on the premise that an individual's problems cannot be understood by focusing solely on the individual's internal dynamics. An individual's dysfunctional behavior grows out of the interactional units of the family, the community, and social systems. Thus, solutions to an individual's problems need to be designed from a contextual perspective.

Incorporating concepts from the client's external world is of paramount importance in my integrative approach. Concepts from feminist, systemic, and multicultural approaches add an essential dimension to understanding how individuals can best change by addressing both their internal and external worlds. In my integrative approach I deal with the systemic (family, community, cultural) variables that contribute to an individual's core problems and draw on these factors as resources to foster the change process.*

WORKING WITH RUTH IN COGNITIVE, EMOTIVE, AND BEHAVIORAL WAYS

See Session 9 (An Integrative Perspective) of the *Student Video and Workbook for the Art of Integrative Counseling.*

My integrative style is a blend of concepts and techniques from many therapeutic approaches. As a basis for selecting techniques to employ with Ruth, I look at her as a thinking, feeling, and behaving person. I work with these three dimensions in an interactive fashion rather than in a linear fashion. Thus, I do not work with Ruth's cognitions, then move ahead to her feelings, and finally proceed to behaviors and specific action programs. All of these dimensions are interrelated. When I am working with her on a cognitive level (such as dealing with decisions she has made or one of her values), I am also concerned about the feelings generated in her at the moment and about exploring them with her. Cognitive and emotive dimensions have an interactive influence on actions. Thus, exploring Ruth's feelings and thoughts need to be connected to how her thoughts and feelings are influencing what she is doing and also what she can do differently. This *doing* would involve new behaviors, which she can try in the session to deal with a problem, and

---

* For further discussion of feminist therapy and systemic therapy, see Corey (2001c, Chapters 12 & 13) and Sharf (2000, Chapters 12 & 13).

new skills, which she can take outside and apply to problems she encounters in real-life situations. As a basis for this integrative style, I draw on the experiential therapies, which stress expression and experiencing feelings; on the cognitive therapies, which pay attention to the client's thinking processes, affecting behavior and beliefs; and to the action-oriented therapies, which stress the importance of creating a plan for behavioral change.

In one counseling session I employ a role-playing technique where I assume the persona of Ruth while she takes on the role of her husband, John. My purpose in doing this reverse role play is to teach Ruth how she can assertively approach her husband and let him know of her desire that they go on a retreat for married couples. We rehearse a number of ways that she could deal with John in the session. Ruth is aware that when she does not get what she wants she has a tendency to shut down. I try to get her to talk out loud, at least in the therapy sessions, when she has a tendency to disappear. Before the session ends, I asked Ruth if she feels ready to deal with her husband in real life. She indicates that she does want to ask John to go on the couple's retreat, and I ask her to design some homework that would enable her to apply the role-playing situations we did in the office to her situation at home.

An integrative perspective takes into account that Ruth is part of a system. To be able to more completely understand her, it is necessary to explore how Ruth fits into her family of origin and the quality of her relationships with her present family. Ruth has identified a number of strained relationships with her mother and father and also with her children and husband. Ideally, we will have at least one session with all of the members of her family of origin. The focus will be on Ruth gaining greater clarity on how her interpersonal style is largely the result of her interactions with her family of origin. The reason for my focus here is the premise I accept that it is not possible to understand Ruth apart from the context of the system of which she is a part. I agree with family therapists who would claim that to understand Ruth's present development it is necessary to go back three generations to see the impact of her family of origin. Most likely Ruth is unaware of how her family of origin is influencing how she thinks, feels, and acts. Lacking this awareness, she drags old baggage into her present relationships, especially with her husband and her children.

If I work individually with Ruth, the emphasis can still be on the many ways her current struggles are related to her family system. By examining her family history, Ruth will learn to recognize the rules that governed her family of origin and the decisions she made about herself. Rather than trying to change the members of her family, we will largely work on discovering what Ruth most wants to change about herself in relation to how she interacts with them.*

---

* For a more complete discussion of counseling Ruth from a family systems perspective and my integrative approach applied to the case of Ruth, see *Case Approach to Counseling and Psychotherapy* (Corey, 2001b, Chapters 11 & 12).

CONCLUDING COMMENTS

Throughout this book I have presented the advantages of constructing a systematic, consistent, personal, and disciplined approach to integrating various elements in your counseling practice. Whatever the basis of your integrative approach to counseling, you need to have a basic knowledge of various theoretical systems and counseling techniques to work effectively with a wide range of clients in various clinical settings. Sticking strictly to one theory may not provide you with the therapeutic flexibility that is required to deal creatively with the complexities associated with clinical practice.

One reason for the trend toward integrative counseling is the recognition that no single theory is comprehensive enough to account for the complexities of human behavior, especially when the range of client types and their specific problems are taken into consideration. Because no one theory has a patent on the truth, and because no single set of counseling techniques is always effective in working with diverse client populations, it is well for you to consider the contributions of the various counseling models and to work toward creating your own integrative perspective. If you are open to an integrative perspective, you may find that several theories play a crucial role in your personal approach. By accepting that each theory has strengths and weaknesses and is, by definition, "different" from the others, you have some basis to begin developing a counseling perspective that fits you.

The notion of searching for new ways of conceptualizing counseling practice that extend beyond the restrictions of a singular theoretical orientation is summarized by Arkowitz (1997), who writes about the contributions, problems, and promises of integrative thinking. In his assessment of the impact of integrative approaches, Arkowitz writes:

> At present, psychotherapy integration has probably had its strongest impact in desegregating the field of psychotherapy, rather than in truly integrating it. Integrative perspectives have been catalytic in the search for new ways of thinking about and doing psychotherapy that go beyond the confines of single-school approaches. Practitioners and researchers are examining what other theories and therapies have to offer. These perspectives have also encouraged new ways of thinking about psychotherapy and change. Further, this has been accomplished without institutionalizing any one way as "the" way. Integration is still an open field in which different ways of thinking and acting are being proposed, explored, and debated. This exploration has already been a healthy challenge to more established ways of thinking about psychotherapy. (1997, p. 256)

10

Working With Transference and Countertransference

Clients bring unresolved feelings with significant others into the therapeutic relationship and project them onto their counselors. Transference occurs in many different kinds of relationships, but especially in intensive forms of therapy. Regardless of whether your theory explicitly makes room for concepts such as transference and countertransference, it is my belief that these factors operate in most counseling relationships.

As you read this chapter, reflect on how you might be affected by the intensity of therapeutic work. I encourage you to remain open to identifying and exploring areas of your countertransference that will surely influence your functioning as a counselor. Being able to deal therapeutically with clients' reactions to you is a major challenge in the client/therapist relationship. It will be imperative for you to recognize and deal with internal conflicts and past pain that are triggered by your work as a counselor.

CONTRASTING VIEWS OF TRANSFERENCE

Transference is common in the therapeutic process, and it is essential that you understand what transference means and that you know how to deal with it ethically and effectively. In developing your own integrative approach, you must conceptualize a way to understand both transference on a client's part and your reactions to the client's transference with you—or your countertransference.

In psychodynamic approaches transference and countertransference are viewed as central to the therapy process. An unconscious process, transference typically has its origins in the client's early childhood, and it constitutes a repetition of past conflicts. Because of this unfinished business, the client perceives the counselor in a distorted way. When such feelings are transferred to the counselor, the intensity of the feelings have more to do with unresolved issues in the client's life than to the present counseling situation. For example, the client may transfer unresolved feelings toward a stern and unloving father to the therapist, who, in the client's eyes, becomes stern and unloving. The client may also develop a positive transference and seek the love, acceptance, and approval of an all-powerful therapist. A central part of psychoanalytic therapy involves the therapist becoming a current substitute for significant others.

Transference allows clients to understand and resolve unfinished business from these past relationships through the present relationship with the therapist. In essence, working through a similar emotional conflict in the therapeutic relationship counteracts the effects of a client's early negative relationships. It is important to be aware of this transference and to be able to help clients work through their feelings in the counseling process. Remember times in your personal counseling when you experienced transference toward your counselor. What was this like for you? What did your counselor do that was helpful to you? If you have not been in personal counseling, think about transference reactions you have experienced toward authority figures, teachers, employers, and supervisors. What were some of the reactions you had toward certain authority figures? What might have been useful to you in understanding and dealing with these reactions so that you could perceive these individuals more realistically?

The psychoanalytic model offers the richest perspective for grasping the implications of both transference and countertransference, and these concepts are a basic part of my integrative approach. Psychoanalytic practitioners consider the transference situation to be valuable because its manifestations provide clients with the opportunity to reexperience a variety of feelings that would otherwise be inaccessible. But transference can be worked with in other therapy systems as well, including existential and Gestalt therapies. I mention this so that you do not get the picture that the only way of understanding and exploring transference in the therapeutic relationship is via the psychoanalytic route. Thinking of transference more broadly, it can be described as any feelings clients project onto their counselor, whether the source of these feelings is in past or present relationships.

Reality therapy, rational emotive behavior therapy, and behavior therapy do not have a framework for addressing transference and countertransference. Reality therapy, as taught by William Glasser (1998, 2000), actually rejects the concept of transference. Glasser contends that transference was created by Freud to avoid getting personally involved in clients' lives. Since the inception of reality therapy, Glasser has consistently maintained that reality therapists should make no effort to be anyone but themselves. He contends that transference is a way for people to avoid taking personal responsibility in the present.

Rational emotive behavior therapists tend to take a dim view of dream work, focusing on the client's past history, expressing and exploring feelings, and dealing with transference phenomena. Transference is not encouraged, and when it does occur, the therapist is likely to confront it. The therapist wants to show that a transference relationship is based on the irrational belief that the client must be liked and loved by the therapist (or parent figure). Ellis (1999) believes devoting any length of time to reliving earlier traumatic situations or exploring transference feelings is "indulgence therapy," which might result in clients *feeling* better but will rarely aid them in *getting* better.

THE CONNECTION BETWEEN TRANSFERENCE AND COUNTERTRANSFERENCE

Your clients will bring past reactions to significant others and place them on you in the present. A client may view you with a mixture of positive and negative feelings, and at different times the same client may express love, affection, resentment, rage, dependency, and ambivalence. Transference can be a path that enables clients to gain insight into how they operate in a wide range of relationships. Clients may experience transference with many people, not just with you as their counselor.

The psychoanalytic perspective holds that it is essential for you as a therapist not only to know your clients but also to know yourself. Be attentive to your own reactions toward clients and how you work with them therapeutically. The transference reactions your clients have toward you will very likely evoke reactions in you as a counselor. These reactions can become problematic if they result in countertransference, which refers to the feelings aroused in you by your clients. In countertransference, your unconscious emotional responses to a client may result in a distorted perception of the client's behavior. Your feelings have more to do with your unresolved conflicts from other past or present relationships than with any feature of the relationship with your client. In the broad sense, countertransference can be thought of as any of your projections that can potentially get in the way of helping your client. It is important to be alert to the possibility of countertransference so that "your problem" does not become your client's problem. However, if you can recognize and monitor your countertransference, this phenomenon does not have to be a destructive aspect in the therapeutic relationship.

WORKING WITH TRANSFERENCE THERAPEUTICALLY

Here are some examples of transference situations you are likely to encounter with clients whom you counsel. Ask yourself what your response might be to a client's feelings toward you, and what feelings are likely to be evoked in you.

CLIENTS WHO MAKE YOU INTO SOMETHING YOU ARE NOT. Some clients will want you to be a parent substitute for them. They may have visions that you will take care of them and solve all their problems. They see you as an all-knowing person who will provide them with answers. Other clients may immediately distrust you because you remind them of a former spouse, a critical parent, or some other important figure in their life. Some clients will not let themselves get emotionally close to you because they feel that as children they were abandoned by people they cared for. Clients who feel their parents did not care for them and who felt abandoned may be leery of letting you into their lives.

CLIENTS WHO BECOME EXCESSIVELY DEPENDENT ON YOU. Some clients may not make decisions without first finding out what you think. They want to know if they can call you at any time. These are the clients who time and again want to run over the allotted time for their session. Dependent clients may view you as all knowing and all wise. They may be convinced that you have the right answers for them and at the same time believe they cannot find their own answers. They are likely to want you to affirm them and convince them that they are special in your eyes.

Be aware of subtle ways that you might foster client dependence. Even though you may intellectually understand the value of promoting autonomy, there may be payoffs for encouraging dependence. For example, if your clients depend on you and tell you how important your input is to them, this can reinforce your need for feeling important and for being needed. Do you have any needs that could be met by allowing certain clients to develop dependence on you? How can you monitor this situation?

CLIENTS WHO ARE NOT ABLE TO ACCEPT BOUNDARIES. Some clients have problems understanding or accepting appropriate boundaries. Much of their behavior within the counseling relationship may be aimed at testing you so that they know how far they can go with you. Some of your clients may transgress therapeutic boundaries and want to enter into a friendship or develop some kind of social relationship with you. Wanting more than a client/therapist relationship can be a manifestation of transference. Perhaps clients want your approval or want to feel special or want to control the direction of the relationship. As children these clients knew no boundaries, and now they are likely to be lost and to feel anxious because they are not certain where they stand with you. In working with such clients, it is essential not to fall into the trap of allowing them to treat you as they did a parent. One way you can do this is by being clear about your own boundaries. Know your role and function in the therapeutic relationship, and avoid relaxing appropriate boundaries to be better liked by your clients.

CLIENTS WHO DISPLACE ANGER ONTO YOU. Some clients will strike out at you with displaced anger. These clients are likely to tell you that because you are supposed to be helping them you have no right to express your own feelings. Don't deny your own feelings or try too hard to "remain objective," but recognize that you are probably getting more of this client's anger than you deserve. Avoid getting into a debate. If you take what you are getting too personally, you are bound to begin to react defensively.

CLIENTS WHO EASILY FALL IN LOVE WITH YOU. Some clients will make you the object of their verbal affection. They may see you as the ideal person and want very much to become the person they see you as being. They are convinced that they could find a resolution to their problems if only they found a person like you who would love and accept them. How might you respond to being the object of adulation? This may be an appropriate time for self-disclosure on your part. For example, if you feel uncomfortable with accolades being showered on you by clients, you can share with them that it is difficult to hear some of what they are telling you. For example, you might say: "I do appreciate your liking and valuing me, yet at times I become uncomfortable with what seems like adulation of me. At times I sense that you perceive me as being without faults. By placing me as high up as you do, it is likely that at some point I will fall far short of your expectations."

These few illustrations of transference behaviors demonstrate how essential it is for you to gain awareness of your own needs and motivations. If you are unaware of your own dynamics, you will tie into your clients' projections and get lost in their distortions. You are likely to avoid focusing on key therapeutic issues and instead focus on defending yourself. If you understand your own reactions to clients, you'll have a better frame of reference for understanding others' reactions to them.

As you reflect on ways that you may be emotionally triggered in working with certain clients, think about how you are affected by those clients you perceive as being especially difficult. How do you respond to the different forms of transference? What kind of transference tends to elicit intense emotional reactions on your part? Do you take intense reactions of a client in a personal way? Do you blame yourself for not being skillful enough? Do you become combative with clients who project a range of feelings toward you?

When clients appear to work very hard at getting you to push them away, it can be therapeutically useful to explore what they are getting from this self-defeating behavior or how what they are doing serves them. You might say to such a client: "You know, I would very much like to work with you. Sometimes I get the sense that you are trying hard to get me not to like you. Are you aware of trying to get me to push you away?" Handled properly in the therapeutic relationship, clients can experience and express feelings toward you that more properly belong to others who have been significant in their lives. When these feelings are productively explored, clients become aware of how they are keeping old patterns functional in their present relationships.

It is a mistake to think that all feelings your clients have toward you are signs of transference. Clients may become realistically angry with you because of something you have done or said. Their anger does not have to be an exaggerated response triggered by past situations. If you are consistently late for sessions, for example, clients may become upset with you over not giving them the time and respect they deserve. Their reactions may well be justified and should not be "explained away" as a mere expression of transference.

Likewise, clients' affection toward you does not always indicate transference. It could be that clients genuinely like some of your traits and enjoy being with you. You can err both by being too willing to accept unconditionally whatever clients tell you or by interpreting everything they tell you as a sign of transference. In short, it is difficult to identify certain reactions as being rooted either in transference or in reality. There is likely to be a mixture of real reactions and elements of transference.

DEALING WITH COUNTERTRANSFERENCE ISSUES

The other side of transference is countertransference—unrealistic reactions you might have toward your clients that may interfere with your objectivity. It is essential that you consider countertransference as a potential source of difficulties that may develop between you and a person with whom you are working. You do not have to be problem-free, but it is crucial that you be aware of how your own problems or countertransference can affect the quality of your working relationships with clients.

Simply having feelings toward a client does not automatically mean that you are having countertransference reactions. You may feel deep empathy and compassion for some of your clients as a function of their life situations. Countertransference occurs when your needs become too much a part of the relationship or when your clients trigger old wounds of yours that may not have healed. Just as your clients will have some unrealistic reactions to you and will project onto you some of their unfinished business, so will you have some unrealistic reactions to them. Your own vulnerabilities will be opened up as you are drawn into some of the transference reactions of those you help.

Although your countertransference has the potential for getting in the way of working effectively with certain clients, this does not mean that all countertransference is problematic or necessarily harmful. Countertransference can have both positive and negative effects on the counseling process. If your own needs or unresolved personal conflicts become entangled in your professional relationships and blur your sense of objectivity, your countertransference reactions will probably interfere with the client's capacity to change. If you use your own feelings as a way of understanding yourself, your client, and the relationship between the two of you, these feelings can be a positive and healing force. Even though you may be insightful and self-aware, the demands of the counseling profession are great. The emotionally intense relationships that develop with your clients can be expected to bring your unresolved conflicts to the surface. Because countertransference may be a form of identification with your client, you can easily get lost in the client's world, which will limit your ability to be a therapeutic agent. If you become aware of certain symptoms—such as strong aversion to certain types of clients or strong attraction to other types of clients—seek consultation, participate in supervision, or enter your own therapy for a time to work out unresolved personal issues that stand in the way of your clinical effectiveness.

Your countertransference reactions can teach you a great deal about yourself. These reactions are not "problematic" or a sign that you are unprofessional. Treat this as an opportunity to learn more about yourself. Be alert to the subtle signs of countertransference and do not be too quick to pin the blame for your reactions on your clients. For example, you may find that certain clients evoke a parental response in you. Their behavior can bring out your own critical responses to them. Knowing this about yourself will enable you to work through some of your own projections or places where you get stuck.

You will probably not be able to eliminate countertransference altogether, but you can learn to recognize it and deal nondefensively with whatever your clients evoke in you. Your own supervision is a central factor in learning how to deal effectively with both transference and countertransference reactions. Your blind spots can easily hamper your ability to deal with "difficult clients" or with your own old wounds. Focus on yourself in your supervision sessions rather than talking exclusively about a client's problem. Spend some time exploring your thoughts, feelings, and reactions toward certain clients. A good way to expand your awareness of potential countertransference is by talking with colleagues and supervisors about your feelings toward clients. This can be especially helpful if you feel stuck and don't quite know what to do in some of your sessions. Part of what could be stalling you are some feelings that you are reluctant to acknowledge.

Ongoing supervision will enable you to accept responsibility for your reactions and at the same time prevent you from taking full responsibility for directions that your clients take. Self-knowledge is your most basic tool in dealing effectively with transference and countertransference. It is well to remember that being instrumental in the changes your clients are making will certainly influence you. If you are unwilling to resolve your own issues, you'll not have much leverage when you challenge clients to work through their transference issues.

SELF-DISCLOSURE IN THE THERAPEUTIC RELATIONSHIP

The traditional model of psychoanalytic therapy discourages therapists from engaging in self-disclosure in the therapeutic relationship. Therapists typically assume an anonymous stance, which is sometimes called the "blank-screen" approach, engaging in very little self-disclosure and maintaining a sense of neutrality. By doing so therapists are attempting to *foster* a transference relationship in which their clients will make *projections* onto them. The assumption is that, if the therapist reveals little and rarely shares personal reactions, whatever the client feels toward the therapist is largely the result of projections associated with other significant figures from the past. These projections, which have their origins in unfinished and repressed situations, are considered "grist for the mill," which is the very essence of the psychoanalytic endeavor.

Many therapeutic models do not call for therapist detachment and remaining anonymous. In fact, person-centered therapy, existential therapy, and Gestalt therapy call on counselors to engage in appropriate self-disclosure as a way of creating an authentic relationship. Indeed, therapy is seen as an I/Thou encounter in which both counselor and client are deeply affected. Many cognitive behavior therapists, reality therapists, feminist therapists, and family therapists make use of self-disclosure as a basic procedure and relationship tool. A certain degree of self-disclosure to your clients is one way to diminish their projections of unrealistic reactions toward you. If you are not a mysterious figure and your clients know something about you, they are less likely to make up scenarios about you in fantasy.

From the person-centered approach I appreciate the emphasis given to immediacy and to an open discussion of how both parties are experiencing the therapeutic relationship. Perhaps the most important type of self-disclosure is the kind of here-and-now immediacy that focuses on what is transpiring between you and your client. This could be especially useful in cases where clients are involved in a transference relationship with you. If you are having a difficult time listening to a client, for example, it could be useful to share this information. You might say: "I've noticed at times that it's very difficult for me to stay tuned into what you're telling me. I'm able to be with you when you talk about yourself and your own feelings, but I tend to get lost as you go into great detail about all the things your daughter is doing or not doing." In this statement the client is not being labeled or judged, but you are giving your reactions about what you hear when your client tells stories about others. Letting clients know how you are perceiving and experiencing them is an important form of immediacy. Selectively discussing some of your reactions toward them may be useful, especially if you encourage clients to discuss the feedback you give them.

Sharing yourself can be a powerful intervention in making contact with your clients. My recommendation is that you monitor your motivations to talk about yourself with your clients. At times clients may evoke feelings in you that connect their struggles with your problems. If your feelings are very much in the foreground and inhibit you from fully attending to a client, it may be helpful for you and your client if you share how you are being affected. For example, you might reveal that what the client is struggling with touches you personally, without giving a detailed account of your situation. Of course, it is always a good idea to explore these personal reactions that grow out of the therapeutic relationship with your supervisor. It may not be appropriate to discuss this material with your client, for you may burden the client with your own problems if you are not careful.

Although I caution against indiscriminately revealing your personal problems to your clients, it can be therapeutically useful for your client if you share relevant aspects of yourself, especially if your life experiences could shed light on their current struggle. It is critical that what you reveal is appropriate and timely, and that it is done for a client's benefit. To determine if your self-disclosures are in the service of a client, ask yourself these questions:

- Do my disclosures help clients talk more honestly and specifically about themselves?
- Does what I share about myself with clients help them put their problems into a new perspective or help them consider new alternatives for action?
- Does my self-disclosure help them translate their insights into new behavior?

Self-disclosure does not mean telling clients detailed stories about your personal past or present problems. Inappropriate sharing of yourself can easily distract clients from productive self-exploration. Sometimes merely letting clients know that you have similar personal issues or similar feelings about a life situation, without going into elaborate detail, is very healing for them. Your disclosure can help them accept some of their reactions as normal and can result in a sense of being understood by you. Admittedly, you are vulnerable when you share your own experiences, feelings, and reactions. Yet can you expect your clients to be willing to be vulnerable in front of you if you rarely show them anything of yourself?

WORKING WITH TRANSFERENCE AND COUNTERTRANSFERENCE WITH RUTH

See Session 10 (Working With Transference and Countertransference) of the *Student Video and Workbook for the Art of Integrative Counseling.*

Ruth displays reactions toward me that can be described as transference. Consider these statements that Ruth made to me in a particular session: "No matter how hard I try, I'm not able to please you. I'm not doing something right. I feel you are critical of me. You are judging me, and I'm not enough, just like with my Dad. I feel that I can't please you or meet your expectations. You must be disappointed that I'm taking so long to get better." These comments illustrate the pattern of Ruth's projections. Because Ruth brought up these reactions, I think there is therapeutic merit in encouraging her to express herself in some detail. At some point in the session I might ask Ruth to explore connections she is making between her father and me, especially if it is apparent that transference is occurring. Exploring her feelings toward me, and what she is attributing to me, can lead to insights regarding unresolved conflicts with father figures that now get in her way.

What about my part in this relationship? If I deal with Ruth's transference reactions toward me appropriately, this can be an avenue of increased self-understanding on her part. However, it is essential that I monitor my potential countertransference. The assumptions she makes about me might well strike a sensitive chord for me, as indeed it did in this session. If I am caught up in my own countertransference, I might respond defensively and become irritated. I am aware that I tend to get impatient and defensive when clients tell me how I am and then treat me on the basis of their perceptions—without including me in this checking-out process. If Ruth continues to make conclusions about who I am and what I think of her without including me in this process, I am likely to feel misunderstood or unappreciated by her. Then I might become caught up in justifying my position or protecting myself. If I am expending a great deal of energy defending myself, I will not be able to deal with Ruth's reactions in a therapeutic manner.

However, in the session under discussion I recognize my own vulnerability and I let her know how I am affected by hearing what she is saying and how it affects me when I feel judged by her. I tell Ruth that I don't think she is giving me much room to be who I am right now. If I can suspend my tendency to convince Ruth that I am different from who she is perceiving me to be, we can work through this transference. If Ruth were to say to me "I can't imagine that you'd want to invest the energy and time in really listening to my pain or really understanding me," I could respond with "I'd like to hear more about how you came to this conclusion about me."

I also engage in self-disclosure and let Ruth know that some of her feelings of "not being enough" touched me personally. Operating on the assumption that I can actually use my personal reactions in a therapeutic manner by appropriately disclosing to Ruth, I tell her: "There are times when I also feel that I am not enough. When I am told how I am, and when I feel judged, this taps into old issues for me. When I am extending myself and feel that I am not appreciated, it is easy for me to tell myself that I am being judged as inadequate." Disclosing this opened up a dialogue that Ruth could use to reflect on her experience in therapy. Later in the session I tell Ruth that I do not always say the right thing, nor am I always as sensitive as I might be. I admit that perhaps some of my shortcomings make it difficult for me to acknowledge the work that Ruth has done in these sessions. My self-disclosure had an impact on Ruth, for she became silent and then got teary. I inquired what it was like for her to hear what I said. Ruth indicated that she was surprised that I was not blaming her and that I was willing to consider my part in how she was perceiving and reacting to me. Ruth was emotionally moved that everything that was going on between us did not have to do totally with her. One of Ruth's fears was that I would tell her that what she is telling me is just about her father. To her surprise, I was letting her know that what Ruth might be feeling toward me has to do with something within me. Furthermore, that we both had in common the struggle with feeling enough personally was affirming for Ruth to hear.

It is critically important that I am increasingly able to recognize countertransference patterns in myself and that I take steps to monitor my reactions. I don't think I need to be "cured" of my personal vulnerabilities, yet I certainly need to be cognizant of the ways my reactions could blur my vision and hamper my effectiveness with Ruth. Through supervision, and perhaps personal counseling, I can learn to identify and accept some immediate reactions that are stirred up inside me when I feel judged or negatively evaluated. It may not be important or appropriate for me to share this with my client, but knowing myself is critical in maintaining a sense of objectivity.

CONCLUDING COMMENTS

I believe personal therapy is essential in your personal and professional development as a counselor. I strongly encourage you to seek the experience of being a client at some time, if for no other reason than to learn to appreciate the courage and persistence it takes to be on the receiving end of the therapy process. This experience can be obtained before your training, during it, or both. In your personal therapy you may experience transference and thus know firsthand how it is to view your therapist as a parent figure. Making use of personal therapy could be an extremely valuable resource, both as a way to resolve some of your personal issues and as way to increase your self-awareness.

Personal counseling can be very useful in recognizing how you may overidentify with certain clients, how you might meet some of your needs at the expense of your clients, and how control issues may be played out between you and a client. I am convinced that to the extent that you have not dealt with your past unfinished problems or unresolved interpersonal conflicts these issues will creep in and color your reactions to your clients. If you have not explored your own pain associated with critical turning points in your life, you are in danger of being carried away on a client's emotional tidal wave.

It is unrealistic to think that you can completely rid yourself of any traces of countertransference or that you can ever fully resolve certain issues from the past. There will always be residual feelings attached to certain events you've experienced in your life, and you will have your own sources of vulnerability. However, you can become aware of the signs of these reactions and can deal with these feelings in your own therapy and supervision sessions.

Becoming a counselor forces you to confront your unexplored blocks related to areas such as loneliness, power, death, meaning, and sexuality. This does not mean that you need to be free of conflicts before you can counsel others, but it does mean that you should be aware of what your conflicts are and how they are likely to affect you as a counselor. For example, if you have great difficulty in dealing with anger, chances are that you will do something to dilute these emotions when they occur in your clients. If you are extremely uncomfortable with conflict and find yourself withdrawing in the face of conflict, it is a good bet that you are likely to find ways to skirt around conflict, even when your clients bring up conflicts they are having outside of the session. If you have not allowed yourself to grieve over some significant loss, you may find it challenging to remain present with clients when they are dealing with feelings surrounding loss and grief. How can you be present for your clients and encourage them to express feelings that you are so intent on denying in yourself?

Personal therapy can be a route to healing your own emotional wounds, and it can provide you with crucial insights into your way of being. If you have avoided dealing with your life issues, you will have trouble being present with clients as they grapple with their struggles. You can take your clients only as far as you have been willing to go in your own life. It is not necessary that you have faced every problem your clients will bring to therapy. How you have dealt with pain in your life and what you have learned from critical experiences is what counts.

Through being a client yourself, you have an experiential frame of reference to view yourself as you are. It gives you a basis for compassion for your clients, for you can draw on your own memories of reaching impasses in therapy, of both wanting to go further and at the same time wanting to stay where you were. Being willing to participate in a process of self-exploration can reduce the chances of assuming an attitude of arrogance or of being convinced that you have "arrived" as a person. Indeed, experiencing counseling as a client is very different from merely reading about counseling theories and techniques. By reflecting on your own experience as a client you can identify aspects of the counseling process that are foundational. You will learn what attitudes and behaviors of therapists actually facilitate working through resistance with clients. This personal and experiential dimension can only enhance your knowledge and skill base in the process of becoming a counselor.

11

Understanding How the Past Influences the Present

Some therapeutic models emphasize that the past significantly influences the present, but others do not. For example, reality therapy, behavior therapy, rational emotive behavior therapy, and cognitive therapy deal with clients' current problems and the factors influencing them. They do not examine the historical determinants of behavior. The premise is that present conditions, rather than traumas or faulty learning during early childhood years, influence clients' problems. Cognitive and behavioral techniques are employed to change the relevant current factors that influence clients' behaviors.

Different therapeutic approaches address the past in different ways. Although psychoanalysis can deal with the present, this approach tends to emphasize not only the past but the relatively distant past. In contrast, reality therapy focuses on the present situation and pays little attention to the past. Gestalt therapy focuses on awareness in the present moment and in the therapeutic encounter itself. Psychodrama includes the future projection technique and emphasizes goal setting and addressing anticipated problems. Sometimes the attitudes brought to the surface in cognitive behavior therapy result in a client's reluctance to change. In these cases it is worthwhile to examine the origins of the beliefs that reinforce these attitudes. This entails some exploration of history and some kind of reconstructive effort. Other clients may be responding largely to role strains in the present and immediate future, and clarifying these concerns is appropriate.

I believe the past is critical in understanding and dealing with a client's present cognitive, emotional, and behavioral difficulties. The psychoanalytic model holds that the shadow of the past can haunt the present, and I continue to see the vital connection between the past and the present in my work.

Typical problems that people bring to counseling include an inability to freely give and accept love; a difficulty in recognizing and dealing with feelings such as anger, resentment, rage, hatred, and aggression; an inability to direct one's own life; a difficulty in separating from one's parents and becoming a unique person; a need for and a fear of intimacy; and a difficulty in accepting one's own sexual identity. From the psychoanalytic perspective, these problems of adult living have their origin in early development. Early learning is not irreversible, but to change its effects we must become aware of how certain early experiences have contributed to our present personality structure. I have incorporated these basic psychoanalytic concepts in my personal integrative approach to counseling.

Although psychoanalytically oriented therapists focus on the historical antecedents of current behavior, it is a mistake to assume that they dwell on the past to the exclusion of present concerns. A common misconception about psychoanalytic therapy is that it resembles an archaeologist digging out relics from the past. Kernberg (1997) indicates that there is an increasing interest in contemporary psychoanalytic therapy to focus on the unconscious meanings in the here and now before attempting to reconstruct the past. Modern analytically oriented practitioners are still interested in their clients' pasts, yet they intertwine that understanding with the present (DeAngelis, 1996). Those practitioners who subscribe to object relations theory view the internal and external world of relationships as central to therapy. Therapy is largely based on the early relations of a child and mother and how this early relationship shapes the child's inner world and later adult relationships (St. Clair, 2000). Therapy consists of weaving back and forth between past and present, between present and past. As the therapist moves back and forth in time, the aim is to understand how early patterns are repeated in the present.

Insight can be a vehicle that enables clients to relinquish old behaviors from the past that intrude into the present. It is useful for clients to understand and use historical data in their therapy, but they also need to be aware of the pitfalls of getting lost in their past by recounting endless and irrelevant details of their early experiences. A preoccupation with the past can be uselessly time-consuming and can inhibit progress, as well as being a form of resistance. Discussion centering around childhood events is less useful than dealing with the past in relation to here-and-now interactions between client and therapist. How this notion of the past applies to the case of Ruth is the topic of the next section.

WORKING WITH RUTH'S PAST, PRESENT, AND FUTURE

See Session 11 (Understanding How the Past Influences the Present) of the *Student Video and Workbook for the Art of Integrative Counseling.*

Dealing With the Past in an Integrative Style

Drawing on my integrative approach to counseling Ruth, I am interested in understanding and exploring (within the restrictions of our time frame) Ruth's early history and assisting her in gaining insight into how her past is related to some of the problems she is experiencing today. I especially like the Gestalt therapy approach to dealing with the past, which brings relevant aspects of the past into the present. When the past seems to have a significant bearing on Ruth's present attitudes or behavior, we bring it into the present as much as possible. I heavily construct my integrative practice around Gestalt therapy concepts as a way to illuminate the connections between the past and the present.

When Ruth speaks about a past event, I ask her to bring whatever feelings surface into the present by reliving them through a variety of role-playing techniques. This is more potent than merely talking about past events. For example, I suggest to Ruth that she *become* the hurt child and talk directly to her father in fantasy. I say: "Bring your father into this room now, and let yourself go back to the time when you were a child. Tell him now, as though he were here and you were that child, what you most want to say." By paying attention to what is occurring moment by moment with Ruth, I get additional clues as to how best to intervene. Ruth may now say all the things she wanted to say to her father as a child but, because of her fear, kept deep inside herself. She might tell her father what she most wanted from him then and what she still wants with him now. The theoretical rationale for most of these techniques is rooted in the assumption that the emotions that were overwhelming to Ruth as a child were dealt with by some form of distortion or denial. By reliving an experience as though it was happening now, emotions that were repressed can come to the surface.

In the supportive, accepting, and safe therapeutic environment, Ruth can allow herself to experience feelings that she has sealed off from awareness, and she can now work through some of these feelings that are keeping her stuck. By challenging her assumptions of how her father is, she is able to establish a new basis for relating to him. Through this process Ruth relives the hurt but has the potential to change it to understanding and resolution. By symbolically dealing in the here and now with people in her life with whom she feels unfinished, she can bring closure to some painful events.

Let's look at a few critical situations between Ruth and her father, along with how I intervened. One critical incident took place when Ruth was 6 years old. She reported: "My father caught me 'playing doctor' with an 8-year-old boy. He lectured me and refused to speak to me for weeks. I felt extremely guilty and ashamed." Ruth may have unfinished business with respect to guilt regarding sexuality that stems from this incident.

To help Ruth explore this past incident and how it still has a current impact, I utilize Gestalt methods. I ask Ruth to role-play by having her be herself (at the age of 6) and talk to me now (as her father). I say to Ruth: "Imagine I'm your father, and I'm not going to say anything. I'll just listen to you. I just caught you with this neighbor boy. Tell me what is going on inside you right now." As Ruth talks to me, I simply listen on the assumption that what is important now is to allow her to express feelings that she has kept to herself for so long. The theme of what she tells me is how embarrassed, ashamed, and sorry she is for letting that happen. She is sure that I (as her father) view her as bad and dirty, that I am greatly disappointed in her, and that I won't love her anymore. It is clear that Ruth is still affected by her past and her rigid upbringing. She is convinced that she did something very wrong in the eyes of her father and her church. She did exactly what she was taught not to do by her church.

Because Ruth brings up the matter of her church, it seems an appropriate transition to move to an exploration of how her religious upbringing has a current influence on her. I suggest a second role play in which Ruth becomes the "voice of her church," the past, and her father. I ask her to talk to me from that stance. For my own part in the role play, I assume the more accepting part and the voice that she would like to hear. Ruth is able to get into her part with gusto, because she is saying aloud what she heard for so many years in growing up and what she has told herself silently. Ruth has incorporated the critical and judgmental voice of her father and the church without really examining the validity of the messages she is receiving from both of these sources. In role-playing the "accepting side," I want to get across that "Even though I have my faults and am imperfect, I am certainly not a bad person." As Ruth's assertive side, a central message I'm striving to get across is that Dad's approval costs me my integrity: "I have been striving all my life, Dad, to get your approval. But to be what you want I have to be scared and always feel guilty. I don't want to do that anymore. To get your approval costs too much."

This gives Ruth an idea of what she would like to be able to say and really believe. Ruth says: "I sure wish I could talk to my father that way!" We devote several sessions to discussion of how Ruth's father played a central role in the moral and religious values that she believed she had to accept to stay in his "good graces." Eventually, Ruth gets the insight that she does not want to live by the religious dogma her father preached, nor does she want to accept for herself the messages he continues to give her about the "right path for living."

The two role plays we do here demonstrate working with both feelings and beliefs that have been an integral part of Ruth's being for so long. The enactment of these role plays brings the past into the here and now and allows Ruth to give expression to beliefs and feelings that have roots in her early childhood. My intervention is designed to enable Ruth to clarify how she wants to think, feel, and believe today.

Along with Gestalt methods, I draw on concepts and techniques from psychodrama to help Ruth understand her past. Although psychodrama is generally used in group therapy, many psychodramatic techniques can be employed in individual counseling. In psychodrama, Ruth would enact conflicts as if they were occurring in the present moment, rather than narrating past events. For instance, I could ask her: "Show me what happened when you were a young child and your father caught you with the neighborhood boy." Psychodrama offers encouragement to Ruth to speak in the present tense and to use action words. Placing the client in the present, regardless of when the scenes actually happened, has a tendency to reduce verbal reporting and turn clients into actors (Moreno, 1987). When Ruth engages in *showing* me what she is thinking or feeling, she moves toward concrete experiencing and cuts through defenses. She will also move away from abstract and impersonal discussions about a topic by plunging into personal enactment of a concern.

A basic tenet of psychodrama, much the same as Gestalt therapy, is that reliving and reexperiencing a scene from the past will give Ruth both the opportunity to examine how that event affected her at the time it occurred and a chance to deal differently with the event *now.* By replaying a past event in the present, Ruth is able to assign new meaning to it. Through this process, Ruth can work through unfinished business and put a new and different ending to that earlier situation.

Dealing With the Present in an Integrative Style

Appreciating and fully experiencing the present is lost on many of us. We ruminate about the past, or we engage in endless thinking about the future. Our minds are noisy, which makes it difficult to be in the moment. As we put our energies toward what might have been or what might be, our capacity to take hold of the moment diminishes dramatically.

Gestalt therapy focuses on the power of the present. Most Gestalt techniques are designed to put clients into closer contact with their ongoing experiencing and increase their awareness of what they are feeling from moment to moment. Just as there are advantages to focusing on the here and now, there are disadvantages to this exclusive focus. Polster (1987) observes that too tight a focus, with a highly concentrated emphasis on the here and now, will foreclose on much that matters, such as continuity of commitment, the implications of one's acts, dependability, and responsiveness to others. In his current thinking, Polster stresses the importance of having clients flesh out their stories, which may include working with the past, the present, and the future.

I am counseling Ruth from a present-centered mind set. Most of our discussions deal with her thoughts and beliefs, her emotional states, and what she is doing currently. Even though I am open to exploring some of Ruth's past experiences, my focus is on examining ways that her past still has a present influence. Ruth and I can direct attention to her immediate feelings as well as her thoughts and actions. It seems essential to me that we work with all three dimensions—what she is thinking, what she is actually doing, and how her thoughts and behaviors affect her feeling states. By directing Ruth's attention to what is going on with her during our sessions, I can show her how she interacts in her world apart from therapy.

Dealing With the Future in an Integrative Style

The technique of making a past situation a present one can be applied to future events as well. The rationale for doing this is the same as working with the past. If the future comes alive through enactment, there is less chance of dealing with abstractions and verbiage. I frequently utilize both Gestalt and psychodrama techniques to assist clients in experiencing their hopes, fears, and expectations for the future. If Ruth is afraid of a future confrontation with her father, I ask her to live her expectations in the here and now by speaking directly to her father in a role-play situation. By expressing her fears and hopes in the safety of the therapy context, she is likely to gain clarity about what she would like to say to her father in real life. Thus, she may say in a role play to her symbolic father: "I want to tell you how much I'd like to be close to you, but I'm afraid that if I do so, you won't care. I'm afraid of saying the wrong things and pushing you even further away from me. Sometimes I think you are so disappointed in me because I haven't become the person you expected."

Psychodrama is also highly useful for exploring some anticipated event in the future. In psychodrama, the past, present, and future are all significant tenses, yet the action is played out in the present moment. Psychodrama can enable Ruth to bring the future into the now: "Show me how you'd like to be able to talk with your father one year from now. Let me be your father and try on some of the things you'd like to be able to say to him."

A technique in psychodrama known as "future projection" can be appropriate in counseling Ruth, especially when she brings up wanting improvements in her significant relationships (with her husband, her children, and her parents). When I ask Ruth to participate in living out a scenario in the future, my goal is to help her express and clarify concerns she has about the future. Ruth's future concerns are not merely discussed but an anticipated event is brought into the present moment and acted out. These concerns may include her wishes and hopes, dreaded fears of tomorrow, and goals that provide some direction to her life. In implementing this technique, I have Ruth create a future time and place with selected people, bring this event into the present, and get a new perspective on a problem. Ruth may act out either a version of the way she hopes a given situation will ideally unfold or her version of the worst possible outcome.

Once Ruth clarifies her hopes for a particular outcome, she is in a better position to take specific steps that will enable her to achieve the future she desires. For example, Ruth can be asked to carry on the kind of dialogue with her father that she would ideally like one year hence. A role-reversal technique can be powerful if used in a timely manner. I might suggest to Ruth: "Let yourself become your father. You know the words you'd most like to hear from him. As your father, speak to me (as Ruth) and tell me what you wish he would say and how you would hope he would act." Through reversing roles with her father, Ruth is able to formulate significant emotional and cognitive insights into the situation involving her father. She can also project herself forward and tell him how she has acted differently toward him during the previous year. If she gets a clearer sense of the kind of relationship that she would like with him and if she accepts her own responsibility for the quality of this relationship, she can begin to modify some of the ways in which she approaches her father.*

---

* For a review of both Gestalt therapy and psychodrama, see *Theory and Practice of Group Counseling* (Corey, 2000). See also *Theory and Practice of Counseling and Psychotherapy* (Corey, 2001c) for more elaborate discussions of Gestalt therapy and existential therapy. For a more complete discussion of ways to work with Ruth's past, see *Case Approach to Counseling and Psychotherapy* (Corey, 2001b; Chapters 2, 3, 4, 6, 10, & 11).

BECOMING THE CLIENT: Examining Your Past, Present, and Future

Reflecting on the Influence of Your Past on Your Present

Most of this chapter has applied the concepts of how the past plays out in the present to my counseling with Ruth. To maximize the applications of these concepts to your own counseling practice, reflect on these techniques as they might be applied to your own situation. Here are a few questions to ask yourself at this point:

- Are there any themes stemming from my childhood that are characteristic of my present existence?
- Are there any unresolved conflicts from my childhood that get in the way of my enjoyment? Do my present behavior or my current problems indicate areas of unfinished business?
- Are there any events that occurred during my childhood or adolescence that I would want to bring into my personal counseling sessions?
- Is there a significant person in my life that I would like to bring into this session by role playing with the therapist playing that person? How willing am I to engage in this type of role play?
- What value do I see in reexperiencing some difficult situation I have been through earlier and talking about how I am feeling in the moment in therapy?

Think of one particular relationship in your life right now that you'd like to improve. Put yourself in the context of being a client in individual therapy. Imagine that you are having a dialogue with that person one year from now. What would you most want to say to him or her? What would you most hope to hear from this person? How valuable do you think the future projection technique would be for you personally?

How Future Aspirations Influence the Present

Your vision of your future has an impact on your present functioning, as does your past. Along with valuing the Gestalt and psychodrama approaches for dealing with the future, I find useful a number of concepts from solution-focused therapy, Adlerian therapy, reality therapy, and existential therapy. All of these concepts would be guiding factors in my work with you.

Solution-oriented therapy eschews the past—and even the present—in favor of the future. It is so focused on what is possible that it has little or no interest in or understanding of the problem. DeShazer (1991) has suggested that therapists do not need to know a problem to solve it and that there is no necessary relationship between problems and their solutions.

The *miracle question* is one way to help you clarify your future goals and strivings. The miracle question technique, designed by deShazer (1985, 1988), might be presented to you thusly: "Essentially, if a miracle happened and the problem you have was solved overnight, how would you know it was solved, and *what would be different?*" I would then encourage you to enact "what would be different" in spite of perceived problems. By formulating this future perspective, you are focusing on what you want in your life and how you can go about getting it.

I very much agree with the Adlerian premise that you can be understood best by looking at where you are going and what you are striving to accomplish. Being influenced by the Adlerian philosophy, I operate on the assumption that you live by goals and purposes, you are moved by anticipation of the future, and you create meaning. My assumption is that the three aspects of time are dynamically interrelated: your decisions are based on what you have experienced in the past, on your present situation, and on the goals toward which you are moving. I appreciate the perspective of the Adlerians, who look for continuity, or a pattern, in life. As you and I look for this continuity in your life, the emphasis is on the goal-directed nature of all your behavior.

From the perspective of reality therapy, it would help to know what your goals in life are. If you decide that your present behavior is not getting you what you want, you are in a good position to think ahead about the changes you would like and what you can do *now* to actualize your aspirations. The present-oriented behavioral focus of reality therapy is a good reference point for enabling you to clarify a vision regarding what you would like to say about your life 5 years hence. Connecting present behavior with future plans is an excellent device for helping clients formulate a concrete plan of action. I believe clients can actually create their own future in this manner.

CONCLUDING COMMENTS

It is one thing to read about the concepts and techniques I've described that are an integral part of my integrative approach, and it is quite another matter to apply them to yourself. The more you are able to identify personal themes of significance associated with your past, present, and future, the greater your chance of coming to appreciate some of these concepts. If you see value in counseling clients from the perspective I've described, you are likely to find ways of using techniques aimed at bringing both past and future concerns into present situations with your clients. If you are reluctant to personally engage in any experiential role-playing scenarios, my guess is that you won't feel comfortable making these interventions with others. Although the emphasis of this chapter has been mainly on identifying and expressing feelings, there is plenty of room for exploring cognitive and behavioral patterns associated with the past, present, and future. I encourage you to reflect not only on the personal applications but to think about the value of dealing with all three tenses in any counseling situation. Remember that who you have been has implications for who you now are. What you are striving to become has implications for the person you are today.*

At this point take some time to reflect about your past, present, and future.

- What are a few of your past experiences that have a continuing influence on who you are today?
- If you could revise one of the chapters of your life, how would you like to rewrite it?
- To what extent has your past given you a greater appreciation of the struggles of the clients with whom you will work?
- In reflecting on your life, what are three aspects of your current existence that you would most like to change? If you were successful in changing these three facets of your present functioning, how do you imagine that your life would be different?
- What kind of life would you like to have five years hence? Are there any steps you can take now to move closer toward your goals?
- How much time do you devote to thinking about your future goals and aspirations? To what degree do you think that your vision of your future has an influence on how you think, feel, and act today?

---

* For a more detailed discussion of concepts I would draw from in working with your past, present, and future, see the discussions of Adlerian therapy, existential therapy, reality therapy, and solution-oriented therapy in *Theory and Practice of Counseling and Psychotherapy* (Corey, 2001c). For a video demonstrating the Coreys' approach to drawing on experiential approaches in bringing the past and the future into the present with members of a therapy group, see *Evolution of a Group* (Corey, Corey, & Haynes, 2000). For ideas for examining how your past choices influence your present and how to establish personal goals, see *I Never Knew I Had a Choice* (Corey & Corey, 1997).

12 Working Toward Decisions and Behavior Change

If you were one of my clients, I would invite you to look at your life as a plan and to evaluate the blueprints that influence who you are today. Existential therapy is the foundation of my integrative approach to counseling, and I operate on the existential assumption that you can be the architect of your own life. If you don't like the design of your present existence, you can take steps to revise the blueprints.

As critical as it is for you to understand where you've come from and to appreciate some of the motivations for your present behavior, I believe this is only part of the story. Understanding the context of your early decisions may be useful in getting a better picture of your development, but self-understanding needs to lead to action if you hope to make significant behavioral change. Insight without action won't help you make existential decisions and revise your existence. This chapter primarily addresses ways of understanding your earlier decisions and increasing your capacity to make new decisions.

Understanding Redecision Therapy

Redecision therapy rests on basic concepts of injunctions, early decisions, and new decisions. Redecision therapy, developed by Mary and Robert Goulding (1979), is a form of transactional analysis (TA) that offers a useful framework for understanding how learning during childhood extends into adulthood. This approach is based on the assumption that as adults people make decisions based on past premises that at one time were appropriate to their survival needs but may no longer be valid. It stresses the capacity to change early decisions and is oriented toward increasing awareness, with the goal of enabling clients to alter the course of their lives. In redecision therapy, clients learn how the rules they received and incorporated as children now influence their actions.

Injunctions and Early Decisions

An injunction is a parental message that tells children what they have to do and be to get recognition and acceptance. Although some of these injunctions may be given in a verbal and direct manner by parents to children, more often than not these messages are inferred: "Don't be separate from me," "Don't be the sex you are," "Don't want," "Don't need," "Don't think," "Don't feel," and "Don't be a child" (Goulding, 1987; Goulding & Goulding, 1979). When you were a child, you decided either to accept these parental messages or to fight against them. For example, you may have heard the message "Don't talk" and decided that you have no voice. Or you may have accepted the injunction "Don't feel" and made an early decision that your feelings are of no value. These early decisions became a basic part of your personality. Many of these decisions may have been appropriate in certain situations in childhood, but they are inappropriate when carried into an individual's adult years. A major part of therapy consists of becoming aware of messages clients may still listen to and the impact of these early decisions.

The decisions listed here are based on an adaptation of the Gouldings' work (1978, 1979) and include common injunctions and some possible decisions that could be made in response to them. As you read each of these messages, and the following possible decisions, apply them to yourself. In growing up, what are some key messages you heard? What are some messages you accepted? What are some injunctions you fought? Have you made any of these decisions? Do you want to consider modifying any of them?

1. *"Don't make mistakes."* If you heard and accepted this message as a child, you may fear taking risks that may make you look foolish. You tend to equate making mistakes with being a failure.
   - *Possible decisions:* "I'm scared of making the wrong decision, so I simply won't decide." "Because I made a dumb choice, I won't decide on anything important again!" "I'd better be perfect if I hope to be accepted."
   - *Reflection questions:* Do you have anxiety about making mistakes? Are you able to welcome mistakes as a way to learn?
2. *"Don't be."* This lethal message is often given nonverbally by the way your parents held (or didn't hold) you as a child. The basic message is "I wish you hadn't been born."
   - *Possible decisions:* "I'll keep trying until I get you to love me." "If things get terrible, I'll kill myself."
   - *Reflection question:* How do you try to convince yourself and others that you are worthwhile?
3. *"Don't be close."* Related to this injunction are the messages "Don't trust" and "Don't love."

- *Possible decisions:* "I let myself love once, and it backfired. Never again!" "Because it's scary to get close, I'll keep myself distant." "It's not worth it to love and risk rejection."
- *Reflection questions:* Do you have difficulty forming and maintaining close relationships? How important are intimate relationships to you?

4. *"Don't be important."* If you are constantly discounted when you speak, you are likely to believe you are unimportant.
   - *Possible decision:* "If, by chance, I ever do become important, I'll play down my accomplishments."
   - *Reflection questions:* Are you able to accept your accomplishments? Do you suffer from self-doubt, telling yourself that your voice does not matter?
5. *"Don't be a child."* This message says: "Always act adult!" "Don't be childish and make a fool of yourself." "Keep control of yourself."
   - *Possible decisions:* "I'll take care of others and won't ask for much myself." "I won't let myself have fun."
   - *Reflection questions:* How much fun are you having in your life? Do you feel that you must keep yourself in check? Are you able to ask others for what you need?
6. *"Don't grow."* The frightened parent who discourages the child from growing up in many ways gives this message.
   - *Possible decisions:* "I'll stay a child, and that way I'll get my parents to approve of me." "I won't be sexual, and that way my father won't push me away."
   - *Reflection questions:* In what ways might you hear internal messages that get in the way of your growth? Are there any ways that you see yourself desperately striving for parental approval?
7. *"Don't succeed."* If as a child you were positively reinforced for failing, you may accept the message not to seek success.
   - *Possible decisions:* "I'll never do anything perfect enough, so why try?" "I'll succeed, even if it kills me." "If I don't succeed, I won't have to live up to the high expectations others have of me."
   - *Reflection questions:* Do you sometimes struggle with feeling that you are enough? Are you able to accept and enjoy your successes? Do you sometimes hear messages that get in the way of your succeeding in an endeavor?
8. *"Don't be you."* This involves suggesting to children that they are the wrong sex, shape, size, color, or have ideas or feelings that are unacceptable to parental figures.
   - *Possible decisions:* "They'd love me only if I were a boy (girl), so it's impossible to get their love." "I'll pretend I'm a boy (girl)."
   - *Reflection question:* Do you ever struggle with feeling that no matter what you do or who you become somehow you still won't fit?

9. *"Don't be sane"* and *"Don't be well."* Some children get attention only when they are physically sick or acting crazy.
   - *Possible decisions:* "I'll get sick, and then I'll be included." "I am crazy."
   - *Reflection question:* Do you ever get attention by getting sick?
10. *"Don't belong."* This injunction may indicate that your family feels that you, as a child, did not belong anywhere.
    - *Possible decisions:* "I'll be a loner forever." "I'll never belong anywhere."
    - *Reflection question:* To what degree do you feel a sense of belongingness?

Understanding the Influence of Your Family

Operating within the mindset of family therapy, I would inquire about the kind of rules you experienced in your family. Family rules may be spoken or unspoken, but they are powerful influencers of how you think, feel, and act currently. These rules, which are often couched in terms of "shoulds" or "should nots," become strong messages that govern interactions within a family.

It is impossible to grow up without such rules. Some examples are: "Never be angry with your father." "Always keep a smile on your face." "Don't bring attention to yourself." "Never let people see your weaknesses; show neither affection nor anger." "Don't confront your parents; always try to please them." "Don't talk to outsiders about your family." "Children are to be seen but not heard." "Have fun only when all the work is finished." "Don't be different from other family members." As a child, you may have decided to accept a rule and live by it for reasons of both physical and psychological survival. When you carry such a pattern into your adult interactions, however, it may no longer serve you.*

APPLYING REDECISION THERAPY TO BEHAVIOR CHANGES

Throughout their writings, the Gouldings stress that early decisions are not irreversible. If you are participating in redecision therapy as a client, it is assumed that you cooperated in making the early decisions that direct your life, so you can now make new decisions that are appropriate and that will allow you to experience life anew. Making an intellectual decision to be different is rarely enough to counteract years of past conditioning. It often helps to employ experiential techniques to go back to the early childhood scenes in

---

* For a more detailed discussion of family therapy concepts that can be incorporated into an integrative model, see Corey, 2001c, Chapter 13.

which these decisions were made. Many of the Gestalt techniques I described in Chapters 7 and 9 can be used to become emotionally and cognitively aware of the impact of earlier decisions and can facilitate the process of redecision.

Awareness is an important first step in the process of changing clients' ways of thinking, feeling, and behaving. In the early stages of counseling, techniques are aimed at increasing clients' awareness of their problems and their options for making substantive changes in their lives. As therapy progresses, clients explore the "shoulds" and "shouldn'ts," the "dos" and "don'ts," by which they have been trained to live. Once clients have identified and become aware of these "internalized voices," they are in a better position to critically examine these messages to determine whether they are willing to continue living by them.

Whatever injunctions clients have received, and whatever the resulting life decisions were, redecision therapy maintains that they can change by changing those early decisions—by making a new decision in the moment. In therapy clients will be challenged from the outset to make new decisions for themselves. Clients are frequently required to imagine returning to the childhood scenes in which they arrived at self-limiting decisions. Counselors facilitate this process with these interventions: "As you are speaking, how old do you feel?" "Is what you are saying reminding you of any times when you were a child?" "What pictures are coming to your mind right now?" "Could you exaggerate that frown on your face?" "What scene comes to mind as you experience your frowning?" "What are you feeling as you describe this scene?"

There are many ways of assisting clients in returning to some critical point in their childhood (Goulding, 1987). Once clients are able to identify an early scene (such as the one Ruth recalled in Chapter 11), it is helpful to allow them to reexperience the scene. Clients might reexperience the scene in fantasy through the use of a Gestalt experiment where some past scenario is brought into the present moment. As part of replaying this earlier experience, it is important for clients to be able to reject the decisions they once made in response to messages surrounding an event.

In this redecision work clients enter the past and create fantasy scenes in which they can safely give up old and currently inappropriate early decisions. Armed with an understanding in the present that enables clients to relive the scene in a new way, they see that a particular decision was the best they could do at a difficult time but that now they can modify that decision. According to the Gouldings, it is possible to give a *new ending* to the scenes in which original decisions were made—a new ending that often results in a *new beginning* that allows clients to think, feel, and act in revitalized ways.

BECOMING THE CLIENT: Experiencing the Redecision Process

I incorporate a number of key concepts of redecision therapy in my integrative approach. I want to explore your injunctions or messages. Such concepts are quite useful in the overall context of understanding how you make certain decisions about yourself and your place in the world. I very much accept the existential notion that what has been decided can be redecided.

Toward the ending phase of counseling, there is considerable focus on examining past decisions and looking forward to making new decisions. At this phase of your counseling, I ask you to review what you have learned about your early decisions as a result of participating in therapy (an approach characteristic of existential therapy, transactional analysis, and rational emotive behavior therapy). To stimulate this review, I typically pose these questions:

- Do you want to revise any of your early decisions?
- Are these decisions still appropriate for you now?
- What new decisions do you want to make?

As you recall from Chapter 6 (on the cognitive perspective in counseling practice), a major cognitive behavioral technique can assist you in understanding early decisions in the form of core beliefs and self-talk. Cognitive restructuring can be incorporated into most forms of therapy. Once decisions and core beliefs have been identified, you are then in a position to critically evaluate these beliefs and decisions and modify them. Through techniques such as cognitive disputing, debating, Socratic questioning, reframing, and cognitive restructuring, you can actively incorporate a sound set of beliefs and a more effective philosophy of life.

The action-oriented therapies—behavior therapy, rational emotive behavior therapy, cognitive behavior therapy, choice theory/reality therapy, Adlerian therapy—all stress the importance of moving beyond the insight and self-awareness levels and taking action to bring about change. The action-oriented phase of counseling is a time for you to solve problems and make decisions. During this time, you and I consider possible alternatives and their consequences, evaluate how these alternatives will meet your goals, and decide on a specific course of action. The best alternatives and new possibilities for action are ones you generate.

Once you become clear about some of your early decisions, you can continue to participate in a wide range of homework activities that will enable you to practice what you are learning in therapy. A major part of the counseling process consists of making new decisions based on the expanded information you have acquired about yourself. By immersing yourself in behavioral homework where you can eventually learn to become your own counselor, you can reinforce this redecisional process. Utilizing an Adlerian technique, I encourage you to act *as if* you are the person you want to be, which can serve to challenge your self-limiting assumptions. I ask you to catch yourself in the process of repeating old patterns that have led to ineffective behavior. It will be essential for you to set tasks for yourself and do something specific about dealing with your problems. In this way, you translate your new insights and new decisions into concrete actions.*

---

* For a more detailed treatment of TA and redecision therapy as it applies to group counseling, see Corey (2000).

WORKING TOWARD REDECISIONS WITH RUTH

See Session 12 (Working Toward Decisions and Behavior Change) of the *Student Video and Workbook for the Art of Integrative Counseling.*

IDENTIFYING FAMILY RULES AND MESSAGES. Ruth and I spend some time identifying and exploring family rules and messages. Ruth comes up with as many family rules as she can recall in growing up as a child. She recollects parental messages such as these: "Don't think for yourself." "Follow the church obediently, and conform your will to God's will." "Never question the Bible." "Live a moral life." "Don't get close to people, especially in sexual ways." "Sexuality is bad and wrong, unless you are married." "Always be proper and appropriate." We spend time identifying and dealing with gender-role messages Ruth still struggles with such as: "Your main concern should be your family." "Don't put your career needs before what is expected of you as a woman." "Defer to what men want." "Always be ready to nurture those who need care and attention."

EXPLORING EARLY DECISIONS. In working with Ruth's early decisions in response to messages that she received from her parents, I borrow concepts from both the psychoanalytic and family therapy models. The psychoanalytic approach emphasizes reconstructing the past and working through early conflicts that have been repressed to resolve these unconscious conflicts. Some approaches to family therapy would posit that Ruth needs to understand family behavior patterns three generations back to unravel patterns and emotional baggage she may have acquired from her family background.

In exploring Ruth's early decisions, I employ a directive and action-oriented approach. Functioning as a teacher, I focus on what she can learn that will lead to changes in the way she is thinking, feeling, and behaving. Once we have identified some of the major messages she has internalized, I will ask her to begin thinking about the decisions she made about herself, others, and the world. I will also ask her to reflect on the direction in which her early decisions are taking her. Ruth sees with increasing clarity that she has lived much of her life in ways that were designed to get her father's approval. She feels that unless she gets her father's acceptance and approval she will not feel good about herself. She reasons that if the father who conceived her could not love her then nobody ever could. If *this* man does not show her love, she is doomed to live a loveless life! Drawing from Adlerian, family systems, and cognitive behavioral concepts, I proceed by getting her to look at themes in her life and by guiding her in critically evaluating some invalid assumptions she continues to make.

At this stage of her therapy, Ruth is increasingly challenging her thinking and her value system, which appears to be at the root of much of her conflict. She is raising questions about the meaning of her life. Ruth is looking at beliefs and values she has accepted to determine if she still wants to base her life on them. Does she want to spend the rest of her life in a futile attempt to "win over" her father? What will it take for her to finally gain her father's acceptance and love?—if this is possible. What might she think of the person she must become to gain his acceptance? Pursuing these questions gets Ruth to *think,* to *challenge* herself, and to *decide* for herself on her standards for living.

Because Ruth has let me know that she wants to reconsider her value system, I have an investment in assisting her in this process. Our counseling involves Ruth in carefully considering what part of her value system she wants to retain and what values she wants to modify. I do not expect her to throw away all that she was taught. The experiential and relationship-oriented approaches emphasize the importance of Ruth critically examining her values so that they become her own. Authenticity consists of living by values Ruth chooses rather than living blindly by values given by others.

RUTH'S EXISTENTIAL QUEST. The goal of our therapeutic endeavor is for Ruth to become increasingly capable of making self-directed choices and influencing the quality of her future through her choices. Ruth is challenged to re-create herself through her projects. Much of our work together involves my inviting Ruth to raise core questions about her existence such as: "Who am I?" "Who have I been?" "Where am I going?"

A basic existential premise that I accept in my relationship with Ruth is that she is not the victim of circumstances. To a large extent, she is what she has chosen and is choosing to be today. For much of her life Ruth has lived a restricted existence. She has tended to see few options for dealing with life situations, and she often reported feeling trapped or helpless. One of my central tasks is to confront Ruth with the ways she is living a restricted existence and to help her become aware of her own part in creating this condition.

I encourage Ruth to reflect on the direction of her life, to recognize her range of alternatives, and to make decisions without any firm guarantees about the future. Once Ruth becomes aware of factors in her past and of stifling modes of her present existence, she can begin to accept responsibility for changing her future. As she recognizes some of the ways in which she has passively accepted circumstances and surrendered control, she can start on a path of consciously shaping her own life and designing the future she wants.

FEMINIST PERSPECTIVE. The feminist therapy model provides me with a valuable lens to understand some of Ruth's core struggles. The intervention of gender-role analysis is especially useful. Gender-role analysis can be employed to increase Ruth's insight about how societal gender-role expectations have adversely affected her and to help her understand how women and men are socialized differently. Through this process, Ruth will learn to identify gender-role messages (verbal, nonverbal, and modeled) she has experienced in her lifetime. With my help she will be in a position to examine the socialization messages she received from society as a whole, from her family of origin, and from her religion. As a result, Ruth will learn that many of her conflicts about her life and identity are due to the fact that she wants to step outside her traditionally defined female gender role. Ruth is now able to identify the positive and negative consequences of following those gender-role messages. Through therapy Ruth learns how she has internalized certain gender-role messages in conscious and unconscious ways. My hope is that Ruth will be able to acquire a full range of behaviors that are freely chosen rather than those prescribed by gender-role stereotypes.*

ENCOURAGING RUTH TO ACT. As much as possible, I structure situations in the therapy session that will facilitate new decisions on Ruth's part. Ruth's redecisions have to be made on both the emotional and cognitive levels, but it is also important that she commit herself to some course of action aimed at changing herself and also bringing about environmental change. Here I like the Adlerian and reality therapy emphasis on getting Ruth to decide on a plan of action and then make a commitment to carrying it out.

Therapy is a place of safety where clients can experiment with new ways of being to see what behavioral changes they really want to make. Ruth has learned that insight without action is incomplete. She must apply the lessons learned in therapy to real-life situations. I consistently encourage Ruth to carry out homework assignments geared to having her challenge her fears and inhibitions in a variety of practical situations. Seeing linkages between the therapy sessions and daily life fits into most of the action-oriented behavioral approaches.

Because Ruth sincerely wants to be different, we use session time for role playing and behavioral rehearsal. Then I ask her to try out her new learning in different life situations, especially with her family. For me, translating what is learned in the sessions into daily life is the essence of what therapy is about. One assignment Ruth carried out was to approach an instructor in the fitness class at her college and request a place in the class as an added student, even though the class was closed. Regardless of the outcome, Ruth is learning that she has a right to express what she wants. Her old style would be to assume that since the class was closed there would be absolutely no way that she could ever add it. This assignment helped her understand that she does not have to give up so soon.†

---

* For a more detailed description of working with Ruth from a feminist therapy model, see the piece written by Kathy M. Evans, Susan R. Seem, and Elizabeth A. Kincade, as well as Pam Remer's work with Ruth from a feminist perspective, in *Case Approach to Counseling and Psychotherapy* (Corey, 2001b, Chapter 10).

† For a more complete description of working with Ruth's early decisions and new decisions, refer to *Case Approach to Counseling and Psychotherapy* (Corey, 2001b): see Donald Polkinghorne's existential therapy perspective on Ruth (Chapter 4); David Cain's person-centered perspective on Ruth (Chapter 5); and John Dusay's work with Ruth from the perspective of transactional analysis (Chapter 9).

CONCLUDING COMMENTS

Ruth is thinking about terminating her therapy. She is starting to think more about getting on with her life without formal therapy. She is learning that she can make new decisions and that she can follow her own voice. It is important to deal adequately with termination issues. The final session will not be enough to accomplish all the tasks for ending the counseling process. Therefore, I ask Ruth to think about what she has learned from her counseling and to develop a plan of what she would like to continue doing when she no longer comes in for counseling. I draw on both the cognitive behavioral and experiential approaches in moving to this new direction in her life. I am asking her to talk about how she would like to feel differently, and to think differently, and what she will need to continue to do behaviorally to make the changes she desires. This consolidation process will help Ruth put a new perspective on what she is taking away from her therapy experience.

I hope you will spend some time reflecting on some of your early decisions and how they extend into your current functioning. After reviewing the list of injunctions and early decisions (pages 125–127), name one early decision you made that you still value and want to retain. Are there any early decisions you made that you would like to examine more fully? Is there a decision about your life that you are willing to revise? What are some of the ways that the injunctions you received and the decisions you made based on these injunctions tend to work *for* you? *Against* you? Ask yourself how your family of origin influenced the kinds of messages that you heard in growing up. How did your family of origin influence some of the most central decisions you have made? In the section on "Becoming the Client" (pages 128–129) I encourage you to act *as if* you are the person you want to be. Let me suggest a homework assignment for one week. Spend a few minutes thinking and imagining the person you want to be. Let yourself identify specific characteristics you would have if you actually were the person you are striving to become. Pick some week that you would be willing to act *as if* you are this person in at least one setting, such as home, school, or work. At the end of the week, ask yourself what is stopping you from becoming the person you want to be. Is there anything you can do to make the changes you most want to make?

EVALUATION AND TERMINATION

Just as the initial session sets the tone for the therapeutic relationship, the ending phase enables clients to maximize the benefits from the relationship and decide how they can continue the change process. As a counselor, your goal is to work with clients in such a way that they can terminate the professional relationship with you as soon as possible and continue to make changes on their own. From your first contact with clients, it is important to convey the idea that your intention is to assist them to function effectively without you. It is not helpful to clients if their therapy continues indefinitely. Basically, the interventions for endings deal with assisting clients in consolidating their learning and determining how they can proceed once they stop coming in for treatment. The tasks of termination include summarizing the counseling experience; consolidating gains; reviewing goals and progress; discussing future work and establishing contracts; and suggesting referrals, if appropriate (Welch & Gonzales, 1999).

I find the action-oriented approaches (Adlerian therapy, reality therapy, behavior therapy, and cognitive behavior therapy) especially useful in providing methods for consolidation of learning and transfer of what was learned in therapy to daily living. Here are some guidelines for you to consider in effectively accomplishing the tasks of therapeutic endings:

- Remind clients of the approaching end of the sessions with you. Ask clients what they'd most like to talk about in the final two meetings with you. At a session prior to the last one you could even ask, "If this were our last meeting, how would that be for you?"
- If you are not limited to a specified number of sessions, and both you and your client determine that termination is appropriate, one option is to space out the final few sessions. Instead of meeting weekly, your client might come in every three weeks. This schedule allows more opportunity to practice and to prepare for termination.
- Review the course of treatment. What lessons did clients learn, how did they learn them, and what do they intend to do with what they have

learned? What did they find most helpful in the sessions with you? How do they evaluate their own participation in this process? It is well for clients to take the lead in addressing these questions. This review and summary process involves both cognitive and emotional aspects. It should also include a discussion of ways to maintain treatment gains and ways of continuing to work after termination.

- Allow clients to talk about their feelings of separation. Just as clients may have had fears about seeking help, they may have fears about terminating the counseling relationship.
- Be clear about your own feelings about endings. You may be ambivalent about letting go of certain clients. Reflect on the degree to which you may need your clients more than they need you. Monitor any signs of countertransference where your needs can make closure difficult for your clients.
- A guiding principle of counseling is attaining client self-directed behavior. Pay attention to clues your clients give about ending the client/counselor relationship and be willing to discuss this at appropriate times.
- Remember that if you are an effective counselor you'll eventually put yourself out of business—at least with your current clients. Your task is to get them moving on their own, not to keep them coming to you for advice. Give clients the tools to become their own counselors.
- Realize that a counseling experience is not aimed at curing all of a client's problems. Counseling is an ongoing and evolutionary process rather than an absolute point of arriving at an ultimate cure.
- Let your clients know of your availability at a future time. Encourage clients to return at a later time should they feel a need for further learning. Clients may need only a session or a few sessions to get refocused. Be sure clients know that asking for help in the future is not a sign of failure but an indication of new levels of strength. Although counseling is best viewed as a terminal process, at a later period of development clients may be ready to deal with a new set of problems or concerns in ways they are not ready to do upon termination.
- Assisting clients to translate their learning into action programs is one of the most important functions during the ending phase. If clients have been successful, the ending stage is a *commencement;* they now have some new directions to follow in dealing with problems as they arise. Furthermore, clients acquire some needed tools and resources for continuing the process of personal growth. For this reason, discussing available programs and making referrals are especially timely toward the end of your work with clients. In this way termination of the professional relationship can lead to new beginnings in a client's personal relationships.

These guidelines are a good start on bringing about a successful ending to counseling. What other aspects would you want to raise with your clients at the final phase of therapy? What goals are essential for an effective and positive ending of a counseling relationship? What are some techniques for closure you would use?*

BECOMING THE CLIENT: Taking Credit for Your Changes

The final phase of your counseling may be a difficult time, and I want to give you an opportunity to fully express your feelings. As a way of thinking about what is involved in positive endings in the counseling experience, consider concepts and techniques that would be useful to bring closure to your experience if you were the client. What do you need to do to summarize your experience, cement your gains, and terminate effectively?

Positive endings include discussing your thoughts and your feelings about your experience in the therapeutic journey. If you are like some clients, you may have some fear that you won't be able to carry into your everyday life some of the central things you learned in therapy. I want you to understand what *you did* to make your therapy experience meaningful.

What you will do once your therapy formally ends is as important as the sessions in the office. Therefore, you and I will spend considerable time talking about what you learned, how you learned it, and what you will do with what you learned now that the counseling sessions are coming to an end. I am especially interested in hearing your perceptions about any changes in ways you think, feel, and behave. I listen to what the counseling experience has meant to you and take my lead from your comments. I ask you at the final session to review specific insights you had throughout the course of your personal counseling. My experience has taught me that many clients tend to forget some of what they learned and to discount the actual value of what they did in their therapy. I want to help you retain whatever you have learned about others, about human struggling, about life, and about yourself. Unless you are able to articulate what you learned through your counseling, and how you learned it, you may not recall key lessons when you need them. I will also ask you what you might do when you experience setbacks or unexpected difficulties. Part of termination is preparing to deal with less than ideal circumstances and coping with obstacles that block your goals.

During our final session, I ask you to imagine your life in some ideal future circumstance, a technique that is used by both Gestalt and psychodrama approaches. I might suggest to you any of the following:

- Imagine that you are coming in for a follow-up session 5 years from now and that we are meeting to discuss how your life has changed. What do you most want to be able to say 5 years from now?

---

* For further discussion of termination issues, see Kramer's (1990) excellent book, *Positive Endings in Psychotherapy.* Also see Welch (1998, Chapter 24) and Welch and Gonzalez (1999, Chapter 18) on completing the counseling relationship and becoming a healer to the self.

- Let yourself fantasize about all the ways in which you want to be different in your everyday life once you leave formal therapy. Close your eyes and carry on a silent dialogue between yourself and the people who are most special in your life. What are you telling them? What are they replying?
- Imagine that a year has passed since you ended your counseling. Also imagine that nothing has changed in your life—that you have continued the way you have always been. Try to picture how you would feel.

During the final phase of therapy, I rely heavily on the cognitive and action-oriented approaches characteristic of the behavior therapies, reality therapy, rational emotive behavior therapy, and Adlerian therapy. I encourage you to continue keeping a journal—writing down the problems you are encountering, describing how you feel about yourself in specific situations, and listing your successes and difficulties in following through with your contracts. Because I feel that an appropriate book read at the right time could be a powerful catalyst in making changes, I encourage you to read as a way of continuing to work on yourself. I suggest that you formulate a contract that will spell out what you will do to maintain your gains and accomplish new goals you are setting for yourself. To implement your contract, I encourage you to continue giving yourself homework assignments.

As the final session draws to a close, I give you an existential message to take with you: "I hope you have become aware of your role in bringing about change in your life. You can assume power by focusing on changing yourself rather than trying to get others to be different. You have become aware of the choices that are open to you; thus, you can now reflect on the decisions you will make. Even if you decide to remain largely as you are, you now are aware that you can choose. Although choosing for yourself can provoke anxiety, it does give you a sense that your life is yours and that you have the power to shape your own future." Finally, I want you to know that you are welcome to call for follow-up sessions if the need arises. Although bringing closure to our work together is essential, I want you to feel welcome to call for future contacts if this is in your best interest.

EVALUATING RUTH'S THERAPY EXPERIENCE

See Session 13 (Evaluation and Termination) of the *Student Video and Workbook for the Art of Integrative Counseling.*

My style of counseling places emphasis on continued assessment by both the counselor and the client from the initial to the final session. Throughout the 13 counseling sessions, Ruth and I discuss her progress in therapy. We especially look at the degree to which she is getting what she wants from counseling (and from me). If for some reason she is not successfully meeting her objectives, we can explore possible factors that might be getting in the way of her progress. At our initial session I made clear to Ruth that a main aim of our relationship is to help her to function without me as her counselor. In our journey together we have been working toward the ultimate goal of Ruth becoming her own counselor.

When is it time for Ruth to terminate therapy? Eventually, the counseling process leads to a time when Ruth can continue what she has learned in therapy without my assistance. Termination of therapy is as important as the initial phase, for now the challenge is to put into practice what Ruth has learned in the sessions by applying new skills and attitudes to daily social situations. During the previous session, Ruth brings up a desire to "go it alone." When she indicates this desire, I am thinking that this signifies major progress. However, we talk about her readiness to end therapy and her reasons for considering termination.

Ultimately, I see termination of Ruth's therapy as her choice. Once she attains a degree of increased self-awareness, has succeeded in making some cognitive shifts, and has acquired some specific behavioral skills in meeting present and future problems, I hope she will begin thinking of ending formal therapy. Becoming her own therapist is a mutually agreed upon goal. To keep her beyond the point where she has made significant changes on many levels could result in needlessly fostering her dependence on me, which certainly would not lead to her empowerment.

In our final sessions Ruth spends considerable time talking about what she learned in her counseling sessions, how she learned these lessons, and what she wants to do with what she has learned now that she will be terminating counseling. This is a good time to talk about where she has been and where she can go from here. Together we develop an action plan and talking about how she can best maintain her new learning. I also share with Ruth my perceptions of the directions I have seen her take.

The focus of the final sessions is on specific changes Ruth has made over the course of her therapy and what aspects of her therapy were most helpful. Ruth indicates that the focus of our work shifted at different times. Sometimes the focus was on Ruth's thoughts, other times on her feelings, and other times on insights she was gaining. At times Ruth needed to simply feel her feelings, other times she needed to take action, and other times she needed to reflect on her beliefs, thoughts, and decisions. From Ruth's vantage point, she has gained a new appreciation for herself as a thinking, feeling, and doing individual.

In Adlerian terms, we are in the reorientation phase. At this time the central task is to encourage Ruth to translate her insights into acting in new and more effective ways. We explore Ruth's perception of her future, and she establishes revised goals. Where does she want to go from here? What are some concrete plans she can put into action? What are some contracts she can establish as a way to provide her with a useful direction? There are a number of options open to Ruth, some of which we explore during the final sessions.

Once Ruth decides what direction she wants to move toward, it is critical that she develop a practical plan of action and commit herself to carrying out her plan. Referrals and suggestions for continuing her growth are particularly useful at this time. For example, now that her individual counseling is ending, Ruth may want to consider joining a therapeutic group. In a group setting she can continue working on interpersonal concerns and can increasingly learn the value of including others in her life. Besides a therapy group, Ruth could also find support in a variety of social networks. Getting involved in some form of social action program, or finding ways she can involve herself to benefit others, could be a most important way to maximize the benefits of her therapy. In essence, she can continue to challenge herself by doing things that are difficult for her yet at the same time broaden her range of choices. If she wants, she could get involved in an exercise class that she has previously avoided out of a fear of how others would look at her body. It is important that Ruth express a willingness to deal with her feelings as they arise in new situations.

One of Ruth's core struggles was with members of her family, and referral to a family therapist may be in order. Ruth might decide to invite her husband and children to be part of a few family therapy sessions. Certainly her changes have not been easy for her husband, her children, and herself. Ruth's changes have implications for others in her family. Even a session or two with the entire family could be instrumental in renegotiating some shifts in roles and expectations. If Ruth does not succeed in bringing about a family session, she can still continue to behave in different ways with each member of her family. Instead of placing the emphasis on changing others in her family, Ruth can focus on herself and relate differently to her husband and children. Indeed, if she presents herself in new ways and keeps the focus on herself, others may be affected by her new way of being.

Evaluating the process and outcomes of therapy is essential. This evaluation can take the form of devoting a session or two to discussing Ruth's specific changes in therapy. I think it is of paramount importance that Ruth be able to recognize what she actually did, both in the therapy office and in her life outside, to bring about the changes she is experiencing in her life. Giving self-recognition and taking credit for these changes is empowering. Her growth is not due to magic on my part, for I am only instrumental in facilitating Ruth's changes. She needs to identify what she specifically did to bring about her process of transformation. If she recognizes her part in her growth, she will be able to continue making positive strides. Here are a few questions to help Ruth appraise the meaning of her experience in counseling:

- What did you learn that you consider the most valuable?
- How did you learn these lessons?
- What can you do now to keep practicing new behaviors that work better for you than the old patterns?
- How can you continue implementing in your life what was begun in counseling?
- Where do you want to go from here? How can you make further plans?
- What will you do if you experience setbacks?
- How will you handle any regression to old ways or temporary defeats?

It is crucial that Ruth and I explore possible stumbling blocks and ways to cope with them. At times, it is inevitable that Ruth will revert to old patterns and experience self-defeating thoughts and behaviors. The point is not that she never experiences setbacks but that she learns to catch herself when she slips into old familiar patterns. As soon as she becomes aware that she is thinking, feeling, and acting in ways that are not serving her well, Ruth is in a position to make a shift and do something different. When she hears her internal critic carping away at her, she can catch this negative voice and shift to a new dialogue. When she experiences depression or anxiety, she will notice this and remain for less time in these states. When she behaves in apologetic ways, she will realize that she does not have to apologize for her existence and she can behave in new ways. The process of catching herself at those times that she becomes ensnared in self-defeating patterns enables her to become her own counselor. Before she entered counseling, Ruth was unaware of these patterns, and thus, they controlled her. Now that formal counseling is ending, Ruth has a greater appreciation that her answers lie within and that she does have the potential to be the expert in her own life. She is realizing that termination of our relationship is the beginning of a new journey.

CONCLUDING COMMENTS

As our journey comes to an end, let me leave you with a few summary remarks regarding constructing your personal integrative orientation to counseling. Remember that designing your counseling approach does not have to be completed by the time you finish this book or this course. A good place to begin is by mastering a primary theory that will serve as a guide for what you do in the counseling process. Select a theory that comes closest to your beliefs about human nature and the change process. Do your best to live a particular theory to determine what aspects of it fit best for you. Look for ways to personalize the theory or theories of your choice. As you have seen, you can get the most from each theory by examining the basic tenets of that theory from a personal frame of reference.

Take the key concepts of several theories that have personal relevance for you and apply these ideas to your own life. One way to do this is by thinking of yourself as a client as you continue studying these theories. What aspects of the different theories would most help you as a client in understanding yourself? In addition, ask yourself what aspects of each theory would be most useful to you as a therapist in working with diverse client groups. As a therapist, what basic concepts are essential aspects of your theoretical orientation? What concepts would most help you make sense out of the work you are doing with your clients? Try to answer these questions by being willing to experience a theory in action and to experiment within the parameters of one or more theories. I have described the concepts and techniques I employ in my integrative approach, both as I worked with you as a client and also with the case of Ruth. I hope this will help you create your own unique style.

Commit yourself to a reading program and consider attending a variety of professional workshops. Reading is a realistic and useful way to expand your knowledge base and to provide you with ideas on how to create, implement, and evaluate techniques. Throughout the book I have provided suggestions for further reading. Take time to review the resources listed in the References and Suggested Readings at the end of the book.

Attend workshops dealing with different aspects of the counseling process and as a way to learn about the implementation of techniques. Just about every theoretical system I've mentioned is associated with one or more professional organizations where you can get further training in the particular orientation. (Consult the Where to Go From Here sections in *Theory and Practice of Counseling and Psychotherapy* [Corey, 2001c] for places to contact for training and supervision of a specific therapy model.)

As you attend workshops, be open to ideas that seem to have particular meaning to you and that fit the context of your work. Don't simply adopt ideas without putting them through your personal filter. As you experiment with many different counseling techniques, avoid using techniques in a rigid or cookbook method. Techniques are merely tools to assist you in effectively reaching your clients. Avoid the trap of fitting your clients to a favorite set of techniques. Personalize your techniques so they fit your style, and be open to feedback from your clients about how well your techniques are working for them.

As you practice, be open to supervision throughout your career. Talk with supervisors and colleagues about what you are doing. Discuss some of your interventions with other professionals and think of alternative approaches you could take with clients. Although it may be helpful to begin by finding a primary theoretical orientation to guide your counseling practice, don't get locked into any one theory. Remain a long-term learner and continue thinking about alternative theoretical frameworks. Be open to borrowing techniques from various theories, yet do so in a systematic way. Think about your theoretical rationale for the techniques you employ.

Don't leave your personal style out of the process of developing your integrative approach. Continue reflecting on what fits for you and what set of blueprints will be most useful in creating an emerging model for practice. Although you will have a solid foundation consisting of theoretical constructs, realize that the art of integrative counseling consists of personalizing your knowledge so that how you function as a counselor is an expression of your personality and life experiences. No prefabricated model will fit you perfectly. Instead, your challenge is to customize a counseling approach, tailoring it to fit you.

It may be reassuring to you that there is no one "right" approach to the integration of counseling practice. Integrative counseling is best viewed as an evolving framework, rather than as a fixed integrative approach. Hal Arkowitz (1997) underscores that there is not one truth to be discovered, but many different ways of looking at our complex world. Arkowitz provides a fitting view of the future of the integrative movement:

> Some who hear about psychotherapy integration are puzzled to find out that there is no single overarching theory of psychotherapy integration that is emerging and that neither is there a single well-defined integrative therapy that characterizes the field. To them, the very term *psychotherapy integration* implies the search for a single integrative theory that ties all of the existing schools of therapy together, along with a well-defined brand of integrative therapy. They are wrong. Such grand integrations in theory and practice are most definitely *not* the goal of most authors in the field of psychotherapy integration. Perhaps the term *psychotherapy integrations* better captures where the majority see it going. Psychotherapy integration is a way of thinking about and doing psychotherapy that reflects an openness to points of view other than those with which one is most familiar. . . . Integrative thinking in psychotherapy has generated new ways of thinking about psychotherapy and change, new ideas that can be tested, and new and useful clinical approaches. In recent years, it has come a long way toward fulfilling its promise. (p. 272)

A FINAL WORD—AND A REQUEST

I hope I have stimulated you to think productively about designing your personal integration to counseling practice. I am sincerely interested in getting feedback from you regarding this textbook, and from the *Student Video and Workbook for the Art of Integrative Counseling*. I'd like to know how this learning package worked for you. I'll welcome and value any suggestions for making this book more useful in future revisions. You can use the tear-out evaluation at the end of this book or write to me in care of Brooks-Cole/Wadsworth, Pacific Grove, CA 93950.

References and Suggested Readings

This reference list represents a carefully chosen group of books that I believe will be useful as resources for designing a personal integrative approach to counseling. Books and articles marked with an asterisk are recommended for further reading.

*ABERNETHY, R. (1992). The integration of therapies. In J. S. Rutan (Ed.), *Psychotherapy for the 1990s* (pp. 19–34). New York: Guilford Press.

*ALFORD, B. A., & BECK, A. T. (1997). *The integrative power of cognitive therapy.* New York: Guilford Press.

ARKOWITZ, H. (1997). Integrative theories of therapy. In P. L. Wachtel & S. B. Messer (Eds.), *Theories of psychotherapy: Origins and evolution* (pp. 227–288). Washington, DC: American Psychological Association.

*BECK, J. (1995). *Cognitive therapy: Basics and beyond.* New York: Guilford Press.

*BERGIN, A. E. (1991). Values and religious issues in psychotherapy and mental health. *American Psychologist, 46*(4), 393–403.

BLATNER, A. (1985). The dynamics of catharsis. *Journal of Group Psychotherapy, Psychodrama and Sociometry, 37*(4), 157–166.

BLATNER, A. (1996). *Acting-in: Practical applications of psychodramatic methods* (3rd ed.). New York: Springer.

BLATNER, A. (1997). Psychodrama: The state of the art. *The Arts in Psychotherapy, 24*(1), 23–30.

BUGENTAL, J. F. T., & BRACKE, P. E. (1992). The future of existential-humanistic psychotherapy. *Psychotherapy, 29*(1), 28–33.

BURKE, M. T., & MIRANTI, J. G. (Eds.). (1992). *Ethical and spiritual values in counseling.* Alexandria, VA: American Counseling Association.

*BURKE, M. T., & MIRANTI, J. G. (Eds.). (1995). *Counseling: The spiritual dimension.* Alexandria, VA: American Counseling Association.

BURKE, M. T., HACKNEY, H., HUDSON, P., MIRANTI, J., WATTS, G. A., & EPP, L. (1999). Spirituality, religion, and CACREP curriculum standards. *Journal of Counseling and Development, 77*(3), 251–257.

COREY, G. (2000). *Theory and practice of group counseling* (5th ed.) [and *Student Manual*]. Pacific Grove, CA: Brooks-Cole/Wadsworth.

*COREY, G. (2001a). *Student video and workbook for the art of integrative counseling.* Pacific Grove, CA: Brooks-Cole/Wadsworth.

*COREY, G. (2001b). *Case approach to counseling and psychotherapy* (5th ed). Pacific Grove, CA: Brooks-Cole/Wadsworth.

COREY, G. (2001c). *Theory and practice of counseling and psychotherapy* (6th ed.). Pacific Grove, CA: Brooks-Cole/Wadsworth.

COREY, G. (2001d). *Student manual for theory and practice of counseling and psychotherapy* (6th ed.). Pacific Grove, CA: Brooks/Cole.

*COREY, G., & COREY, M. (1997). *I never knew I had a choice* (6th ed.). Pacific Grove, CA: Brooks/Cole.

COREY, G., COREY, M., CALLANAN, P., & RUSSELL, J. M. (1992). *Group techniques* (2nd ed.). Pacific Grove, CA: Brooks/Cole.

COREY, G., COREY, M., & HAYNES, R. (1998). *Ethics in action: Student video and workbook.* Pacific Grove, CA: Brooks/Cole.

COREY, G., COREY, M., & HAYNES, R. (2000). *Evolution of a group: Student video and workbook.* Pacific Grove, CA: Brooks-Cole/Wadsworth.

COREY, M., & COREY, G. (1997). *Groups: Process and practice* (5th ed.). Pacific Grove, CA: Brooks/Cole.

COREY, M., & COREY, G. (1998). *Becoming a helper* (3rd ed.). Pacific Grove, CA: Brooks/Cole.

CORSINI, R. J., & WEDDING, D. (Eds.). (1995). *Current psychotherapies* (5th ed.). Itasca, IL: F. E. Peacock.

*DATTILIO, F. M., & FREEMAN, A. (1992). Introduction to cognitive therapy. In A. Freeman & E. M. Dattilio (Eds.), *Comprehensive casebook of cognitive therapy* (pp. 3–11). New York: Plenum.

DeANGELIS, T. (1996). Psychoanalysis adapts to the 1990s. *APA Monitor, 27*(9), 1, 43.

DeSHAZER, S. (1985). *Keys to solutions in brief therapy.* New York: Norton.

DeSHAZER, S. (1988). *Clues: Investigating solutions in brief therapy.* New York: Norton.

DeSHAZER, S. (1991). *Putting difference to work.* New York: Norton.

DREIKURS, R. (1997). Holistic medicine. *Individual Psychology, 53*(2), 127–205.

ELLIS, A. (1999). *How to make yourself happy and remarkably less disturbable.* Atascadero, CA: Impact Publishers.

*ELLIS, A., & MacLAREN, C. (1998). *Rational emotive behavior therapy: A therapist's guide.* San Luis Obispo, CA: Impact Publishers.

FUKUYAMA, M. A. (1990). Taking a universal approach to multicultural counseling. *Counselor Education and Supervision, 30*(1), 6–17.

GILLILAND, B. E., & JAMES, R. K. (1998). *Theories and strategies in counseling and psychotherapy.* Boston: Allyn & Bacon.

*GLASSER, W. (1998). *Choice theory: A new psychology of personal freedom.* New York: HarperCollins.

*GLASSER, W. (2000). *Reality therapy in action.* New York: HarperCollins.

GOLDFRIED, M. R., & CASTONGUAY, L. G. (1992). The future of psychotherapy integration. *Psychotherapy, 29*(l), 4–10.

*GOLDFRIED, M. R., CASTONGUAY, L. G., & SAFRAN, J. D. (1992). Core issues and future directions in psychotherapy. In J. C. Norcross & M. R. Goldfried (Eds.), *Handbook of psychotherapy integration* (pp. 593–616). New York: Basic Books.

*GOULDING, M. M. (1987). Transactional analysis and redecision therapy. In J. K. Zeig (Ed.), *The evolution of psychotherapy* (pp. 285–299). New York: Brunner/Mazel.

*GOULDING, M., & GOULDING, R. (1979). *Changing lives through redecision therapy.* New York: Brunner/Mazel.

GOULDING, R., & GOULDING, M. (1978). *The power is in the patient.* San Francisco: TA Press.

*GREENBERG, L. S., RICE, L. N., & ELLIOTT, R. (1993). *Facilitating emotional change: The moment-by-moment process.* New York: Guilford Press.

*HINTERKOPF, E. (1998). *Integrating spirituality in counseling: A manual for using the experiential focusing method.* Alexandria, VA: American Counseling Association.

IVEY, A. E., IVEY, M. B., & SIMEK-MORGAN, L. (1997). *Counseling and psychotherapy: A multicultural perspective.* Boston: Allyn & Bacon.

JENSEN, J. P., & BERGIN, A. E. (1988). Mental health values of professional therapists: A national interdisciplinary survey. *Professional Psychology: Research and Practice, 19*(3), 290–297.

KERNGERG, O. F. (1997). Convergences and divergences in contemporary psychoanalytic technique and psychoanalytic psychotherapy. In J. K. Zeig (Ed.), *The evolution of psychotherapy: The third conference* (pp. 3–22). New York: Brunner/Mazel.

KELLY, E. W. (1995). *Spirituality and religion in counseling and psychotherapy: Diversity in theory and practice.* Alexandria, VA: American Counseling Association.

KRAMER, S. A. (1990). *Positive endings in psychotherapy: Bringing meaningful closure to therapeutic relationships.* San Francisco: Jossey-Bass.

*LAZARUS, A. A. (1989). *The practice of multimodal therapy.* Baltimore: Johns Hopkins University Press.

LAZARUS, A. A. (1992). Multimodal therapy: Technical eclecticism with minimal integration. In J. C. Norcross & M. R. Goldfried (Eds.), *Handbook of psychotherapy integration* (pp. 231–263). New York: Basic Books.

*LAZARUS, A. A. (1995). Different types of eclecticism and integration: Let's be aware of the dangers. *Journal of Psychotherapy Integration, 5*(1), 27–39.

LAZARUS, A. A. (1996a). Some reflections after 40 years of trying to be an effective psychotherapist. *Psychotherapy, 33*(1), 142–145.

*LAZARUS, A. A. (1996b). The utility and futility of combining treatments in psychotherapy. *Clinical Psychology: Science and Practice, 3*(1), 59–68.

*LAZARUS, A. A. (1997a). *Brief but comprehensive psychotherapy: The multimodal way.* New York: Springer.

LAZARUS, A. A.. (1997b). Can psychotherapy be brief, focused, solution-oriented, and yet comprehensive? A personal evolutionary perspective. In J. K. Zeig (Ed.), *The evolution of psychotherapy: The third conference* (pp. 83–94). New York: Brunner/Mazel.

*LAZARUS, A. A., & BEUTLER, L. E. (1993). On technical eclecticism. *Journal of Counseling and Development, 71*(4), 381–385.

*LAZARUS, A. A., BEUTLER, L. E., & NORCROSS, J. C. (1992). The future of technical eclecticism. *Psychotherapy, 29*(1), 11–20.

LOCKE, D. C. (1990). A not so provincial view of multicultural counseling. *Counselor Education and Supervision, 30*(1), 18–25.

MARTIN, J. E., & BOOTH, J. (1999). Behavioral approaches to enhance spirituality. In W. R. Miller (Ed.), *Integrating spirituality into treatment: Resources for practitioners* (pp. 161–175). Washington, DC: American Psychological Association.

MAY, R., & YALOM, I. (1995). Existential psychotherapy. In R. J. Corsini & D. Wedding (Eds.), *Current psychotherapies* (5th ed., pp. 262–292). Itasca, IL: F. E. Peacock.

MILLER, W. R. (1999a). Diversity training in spiritual and religious issues. In W. R. Miller (Ed.), *Integrating spirituality into treatment: Resources for practitioners* (pp. 253–263). Washington, DC: American Psychological Association.

*MILLER, W. R. (Ed.). (1999b). *Integrating spirituality into treatment: Resources for practitioners.* Washington, DC: American Psychological Association.

MILLER, W. R., & THORESEN, C. E. (1999). Spirituality and health. In W. R. Miller (Ed.), *Integrating spirituality into treatment: Resources for practitioners* (pp. 3–18). Washington, DC: American Psychological Association.

MIRANTI, J., & BURKE, M. T. (1995). Spirituality: An integrated component of the counseling process. In M. T. Burke & J. G. Miranti (Eds.), *Counseling: The spiritual dimension* (pp. 1–3). Alexandria, VA: American Counseling Association.

MORENO, Z. T. (1987). Psychodrama, role theory, and the concept of the social atom. In J. K. Zeig (Ed.), *The evolution of psychotherapy* (pp. 341–366). New York: Brunner/Mazel.

MORGAN, B., & MacMILLAN, P. (1999). Helping clients move toward constructive change: A three-phase integrative counseling model. *Journal of Counseling and Development, 77*(2), 153–159.

*MOULTON, P., & HARPER, L. (1999). *Outside looking in: When someone you love is in therapy.* Brandon, VT: Safer Society Press.

*NORCROSS, J. C., & GOLDFRIED, M. R. (Eds.). (1992). *Handbook of psychotherapy integration.* New York: Basic Books.

NORCROSS, J. C., & NEWMAN, C. F. (1992). Psychotherapy integration: Setting the context. In J. C. Norcross & M. R. Goldfried (Eds.), *Handbook of psychotherapy integration* (pp. 3–45). New York: Basic Books.

NYSTUL, M. (1999a). An interview with Gerald Corey. *The Journal of Individual Psychology, 55*(1), 15–25.

NYSTUL, M. (1999b). An interview with Paul Pedersen. *The Journal of Individual Psychology, 55*(2), 216–224.

PATTERSON, C. H., & WATKINS, C. E. (1996). *Theories of psychotherapy* (5th ed.). New York: HarperCollins.

PAUL, G. L. (1967). Outcome research in psychotherapy. *Journal of Consulting Psychology, 31,* 109–188.

PEDERSEN, P. (1997). *Culture-centered counseling interventions: Striving for accuracy.* Thousand Oaks, CA: Sage.

*PEDERSEN, P. (2000). *A handbook for developing multicultural awareness* (3rd ed.). Alexandria, VA: American Counseling Association.

POLSTER, E. (1987). Escape from the present: Transition and storyline. In J. K. Zeig (Ed.), *The evolution of psychotherapy* (pp. 326–340). New York: Brunner/Mazel.

*PRESTON, J. (1998). *Integrative brief therapy: Cognitive, psychodynamic, humanistic and neurobehavioral approaches.* San Luis Obispo, CA: Impact Publishers.

*PROCHASKA, J. O., & NORCROSS, J. C. (1999). *Systems of psychotherapy: A transtheoretical analysis* (4th ed.). Pacific Grove, CA: Brooks/Cole.

*RICHARDS, P. S., & BERGIN, A. E. (1997). *A spiritual strategy for counseling and psychotherapy.* Washington, DC: American Psychological Association.

*RICHARDS, P. S., RECTOR, J. M., & TJELTVEIT, A. C. (1999). Values, spirituality, and psychotherapy. In W. R. Miller (Ed.), *Integrating spirituality into treatment: Resources for practitioners* (pp. 133–160). Washington, DC: American Psychological Association.

ST. CLAIR, M. (2000). *Object relations and self psychology: An introduction* (3rd ed.). Pacific Grove, CA: Brooks/Cole.

*SHAFRANSKE, E. P. (Ed.). (1996). *Religion and the clinical practice of psychology.* Washington, DC: American Psychological Association.

SHARF, R. S. (2000). *Theories of psychotherapy and counseling: Concepts and cases.* Pacific Grove, CA: Brooks-Cole/Wadsworth.

SUE, D. W., IVEY, A., & PEDERSEN, P. (1996). *A theory of multicultural counseling and therapy.* Pacific Grove, CA: Brooks/Cole.

SUE, D. W., & SUE, D. (1999). *Counseling the culturally different: Theory and practice* (3rd ed.). New York: Wiley.

*VONTRESS, C. E., JOHNSON, J. A., & EPP, L. R. (1999). *Cross-cultural counseling: A casebook.* Alexandria, VA: American Counseling Association.

WATTS, R. E. (1999). The vision of Adler: An introduction. In R. E. Watts & J. Carlson (Eds.), *Interventions and strategies in counseling and psychotherapy* (pp. 1–13). Philadelphia, PA: Accelerated Development (Taylor & Francis Group).

WATTS, R. E., & CARLSON, J. (Eds.). (1999). *Interventions and strategies in counseling and psychotherapy.* Philadelphia, PA: Accelerated Development (Taylor & Francis Group).

*WELCH, I. D. (1998). *The path of psychotherapy: Matters of the heart.* Pacific Grove, CA: Brooks/Cole.

*WELCH, I. D., & GONZALEZ, D. M. (1999). *The process of counseling and psychotherapy: Matters of skill.* Pacific Grove, CA: Brooks/Cole.

WOLFERT, R., & COOK, C. A. (1999). Gestalt therapy in action. In D. J. Wiener (Ed.), *Beyond talk therapy: Using movement and expressive techniques in clinical practice* (pp. 3–27). Washington, DC: American Psychological Association.

*WUBBOLDING, R. E. (2000). *Reality therapy for the 21st century.* Muncie, IN: Accelerated Development (Taylor & Francis).